Personalizing the HIGH SCHOOL EXPERIENCE for Each Student

Personalizing the HIGH SCHOOL EXPERIENCE

for Each Student

Joseph DiMartino

John H. Clarke

ASCD

Association for Supervision and Curriculum Development • Alexandria, Virginia USA

Association for Supervision and Curriculum Development
1703 N. Beauregard St. • Alexandria, VA 22311-1714 USA
Phone: 800-933-2723 or 703-578-9600 • Fax: 703-575-5400
Web site: www.ascd.org • E-mail: member@ascd.org
Author guidelines: www.ascd.org/write

Gene R. Carter, *Executive Director*; Nancy Modrak, *Publisher*; Julie Houtz, *Director of Book Editing &*
Production; Deborah Siegel, *Project Manager*; Georgia Parks, *Senior Graphic Designer*; Mike Kalyan,
Production Manager; Carmen Yuhas, *Production Specialist*; Keith Demmons, *Desktop Publishing*
Specialist.

PAPERBACK ISBN: 978-1-4166-0647-5 ASCD product #107054   s4/08
Also available as an e-book through ebrary, netLibrary, and many online booksellers (see Books in
Print for the ISBNs).

Quantity discounts for the paperback edition only: 10–49 copies, 10%; 50+ copies, 15%; for 1,000
or more copies, call 800-933-2723, ext. 5634, or 703-575-5634. For desk copies: member@ascd.org.

Library of Congress Cataloging-in-Publication Data

DiMartino, Joseph.
  Personalizing the high school experience for each student / Joseph DiMartino and John H. Clarke.
      p. cm.
  Includes bibliographical references and index.
  ISBN 978-1-4166-0647-5 (pbk. : alk. paper) 1. Individualized instruction--United States. 2.
High school teaching--United States. I. Clarke, John H., 1943- II. Title.

  LB1031.D56 2008
  373.139'4--dc22

                        2007046824

18 17 16 15 14 13 12 11 10 09 08   1 2 3 4 5 6 7 8 9 10 11 12

Personalizing the High School Experience for Each Student

1

A FAILURE TO ADAPT

THEY'RE NOT STUPID

"I'm not stupid!"

That comment represents one of the most heart wrenching and memorable conversations of my life.

It's a quote from my son Erick. Erick was adopted, along with his half brother, Mauricio, from Guatemala when he was 8 years old. The boys' arrival expanded the number of children in our family to six. While two of our other children were also adopted, the addition of Mauricio and Erick exposed the woefully inadequate education experience that immigrant students are subjected to in this country.

When Mauricio, then 12, enrolled in the 5th grade English as a second language (ESL) program and Erick enrolled in the 1st grade ESL program, we became aware of an equity gap that was systemic and abusive. We had been assured that the ESL program was academically rigorous and appropriately personalized for the students, who represented nearly a dozen different cultures and languages.

To our dismay, we discovered the contrary to be true. The program was neither personalized nor rigorous. In our first visit to the school, we discovered that Erick was in a classroom in the basement that had been the locker room when I had attended junior high in the same building. More appalling was Mauricio's room, which had been the lumber storage closet for the woodshop when the building was a junior high. The textbooks on display were decades old and had covers and pages missing.

My wife, Pat, and I became very concerned, so I went to the school to observe their classes the next day. Mauricio was in a class with 18 other 4th, 5th, and 6th graders crammed into the former storage closet. They had a dedicated teacher struggling to educate this group of students who were from Europe, Asia, Latin America, and Africa, and who spoke Portuguese, Polish, Russian, Italian, Korean, and Spanish. Erick's class had a little more space but more students—about 30 in the 1st, 2nd, and 3rd grades. At the end of the school day, I had a long conversation with both of those teachers, who were struggling to educate their students in all the core subjects with little support from the building or district administration.

After this discovery, I went through the local channels to address the inequities that I saw. I met with the building principal, who felt that his hands were tied by the district. So, I met with the superintendent, who subsequently asked the district director of special populations to conduct a study of the situation. The study was immediately carried out, and the conclusions were bizarre, to say the least. The report concluded that each of the two classrooms required the addition of two paraprofessionals— one who could speak Portuguese and one who could speak Spanish—so that instruction could be personalized. Because the classroom conditions were so crowded, however, the report concluded that adding the paraprofessionals would increase the noise level in such a confined space, and therefore the final recommendation was to do nothing!

Now incensed, I approached the local school board. Remember, this was my town, and I knew each of the board members personally. They listened politely and refused to change anything to improve the conditions for these students. So, I then filed class action discrimination appeals to both the state and federal offices for civil rights. Miraculous things happened when the district office learned that it was being investigated by the U.S. Department of Education. Books arrived. The paraprofessionals were hired. A new director of special populations, who was committed to doing things differently, was also hired.

The program was changed so that Erick was able to improve his learning and gradually achieve to the point that when he was leaving 6th grade, he was considered a pretty good student. In fact, at the school's graduation banquet for the 6th grade students and their parents, the principal chose to read Erick's essay, "Coming to America." Many parents had tears in their eyes. We were understandably proud of Erick and thought that good things lay ahead for him in his education. Unfortunately, that night turned out to be the high point of Erick's public school education.

We were then—and still are—firm believers in public education. My father, myself, my four siblings, and our five other children had all graduated from the local public high school, and we were certain that Erick would as well. In addition, I was employed at the Rhode Island Department of Education and worked part-time in our town as the boys' high school soccer coach.

Despite our constant advocacy and cajoling, Erick started on a downward spiral when he entered junior high. Things got really bad when he became a high school freshman. He started to run from the school at every opportunity. He was a great athlete, but the carrot of athletic eligibility didn't sufficiently entice him to engage in learning. We were involved in countless school meetings with Erick and his teachers and administrators. At one of those meetings, I tired of the accusation that we weren't doing everything possible to get him to attend school. I declared: "We are doing everything possible to get Erick to come to school. The one thing we can't do is get him to like it here. But *you* could do that if you tried!" Although making that statement helped me feel good, it didn't do anything to help Erick's situation. These events are so strongly etched in my memory that I still cringe when I hear educators blame parents for students' lack of engagement.

Erick didn't earn very many credits in his first year in high school. As a result, he had to repeat the 9th grade. During this repeat year, I encouraged Erick to look into applying to some private schools that might better address his personality. He refused. So, we had another tough year, and once again he didn't earn enough credits to become a sophomore.

During his third year as a freshman, Erick asked me if he could look into private schools. Needless to say, we were ecstatic for Erick—but certainly disappointed that our community was incapable of providing him with an adequate education. After doing some research, Erick chose Saint Andrews, a small private school in Barrington, Rhode Island, that focused on students who weren't successful in the typical public high school environment.

A month after Erick began at Saint Andrews, he came into our sitting room and made this memorable statement: "I'm not stupid!"

We responded almost in unison, "We know that, Erick."

"I really mean it. I'm not stupid."

"We really mean it. We know that."

"Then why did they make me feel so stupid at the other high school?"

The silence in the room was palpable. Pat and I were speechless. We had not realized the profoundly negative view that resulted from his earlier high school experience.

Since that memorable day, I have pondered this brief conversation often. Why had Erick felt so stupid? I knew the teachers well enough to know that they didn't intend to make him feel that way. What was it about Saint Andrews that made him feel so smart? I came to some unmistakable conclusions.

Saint Andrews was a small school where every student was known and known well. Saint Andrews had a student advisory program where each student met with his or her advisor twice a day—once in the morning before the start of school and once at the end of the day to check in. The advisor spoke with each of Erick's content area teachers every two weeks to see how he was doing and reviewed that progress with Erick, before calling me or Pat to update us. Saint Andrews had a modified block schedule that allowed Erick to engage in hands-on learning activities that gave him a chance to shine. The school required every student to participate in athletics or a club. A teacher in the school coached each team, so the personalization connections extended to the playing field and other activities. For the first time since 6th grade, Erick was given literacy instruction that allowed him to improve his writing skills. None of these things happened for any students at our public high school.

But I am convinced that the teachers and administrators at our school didn't realize the effect that the school organization and culture had on so many students who, like Erick, struggled to learn in a classroom where instruction delivered through lecture was the norm. After two years at Saint Andrews, Erick graduated and was accepted and enrolled in a four-year college. Of the 30 or so children who were in the ESL class with Erick when he started school in the 1st grade, only one other student made it all the way to graduate from high school. I knew most of those kids, and I know that they included many gifted students who, like Erick, were never able to connect their wisdom to their high school's classes.

—*Joseph DiMartino*

◆ ◆

Problem Areas for High Schools

How could it be that a public high school should create experiences meant to develop individual capability—and yet teach Erick that he was stupid? In research over the last decade, educators have learned to see six areas in which high schools begin to fail their students:

• *Depersonalization.* Because managing adolescents and young adults in one building is overwhelming, high schools offer few options that appeal to young people with distinctive interests, talents, and aspirations. Yet young people come to high school hoping to forge a unique identity.

• *Lack of adult support.* High school students spend a great deal more time talking with their friends than with a caring adult who knows them well. Young people follow their peers because they do not see any alternative.

• *Unresponsive teaching.* Facing more than 100 students each day, teachers use the same plan for all students, even when those students are characterized by vast differences.

• *Imperceptible results.* Particularly when a student does not earn good grades, the rewards for being in school remain elusive. Students want to see that they are making progress—toward common standards and their own goals.

• *Invisibility.* Only the most notable students, leaders, and athletes (and troublemakers) earn recognition beyond a small group of friends.

Yet high school students crave the recognition of others, even as they dread public exposure.

- *Isolation.* High schools are designed to protect young people from exploitation by the adult world—at the same time that they aim to prepare students for adult roles. High school students need opportunities to engage the larger community so they can aim their education toward a clear purpose.

These six problem areas organize this book, allowing us to look at personalized learning in several different ways and offering six ways to engage students and prevent any from believing they are stupid.

Turnaround in a Smaller School

Over the past decade, many observers have come to realize that the conditions that Erick faced in our high school are the norm throughout the United States. We are constantly being bombarded with evidence that our high schools are failing. The Bill & Melinda Gates Foundation keeps reminding us that one-third of our entering 9th graders won't graduate, another one-third will graduate unprepared for the postsecondary experience, and only one-third will graduate from high school prepared for success after graduation. The Organization for Economic Cooperation and Development (OECD), through its global surveys, has pointed out that we have gone from having the highest percentage of high school completers in the world to 16th. OECD presents evidence that more and more of the industrialized nations are passing us. And, in the Programme for International Student Assessment (PISA) in math for high-school-aged youth, the average U.S. performance was statistically lower than that of 20 of the 30 OECD countries that participated in the PISA and statistically higher than only Portugal, Italy, Greece, Mexico, and Turkey. Further, because of the speed of communications today, jobs that used to require U.S. employees can now be carried out in India or China (OECD, 2006).

How did we get into this mess?

Replacing an American Institution

Many critics believe that the high school is broken and that the people who work in high schools are lazy or incapable. We believe that the high school isn't broken. Rather, it is obsolete. The basic design of our high schools is a century old and no longer appropriate for educating American youth.

In the 1890s, Harvard College, a regional institute of higher education, desired to become a national university. To guide Harvard leaders in how to do this and to ensure that they would be getting students from across the country who were properly prepared to be successful in higher education, the college convened the Carnegie Commission. Yes, we're talking about that Carnegie Commission—the commission that decided that our high school students needed to earn course credits based on seat time. This 19th century concept, which is based solely on educating students who would be able to go on to Harvard, is still the basic organizing structure of our high schools in the 21st century.

The United States in the 1890s was a country whose population felt that an education past the 4th grade was a waste of time for most individuals. It was a country where high school was only for those who needed the connection between elementary school and higher education. It was a country where very few women and at most 5 percent of the young men went to college. That's who our high schools were designed to educate: 5 percent of our young men. The rest of our adolescents were employed in our mills, mines, and farms.

The dedicated educators in this country have been able to make the high school designed to meet the needs of 5 percent of the young men work reasonably well for about one-third of our current students. This adaptation has taken a superhuman effort by our high school educators, but the world has changed dramatically in the past century. The economic imperative for our society is compelling enough. But, when you consider that we are the world's premier democracy, we need to be preparing all students not just to keep our economic engine running, but also to become contributing citizens in an increasingly complex democracy.

If we assume that our high schools are broken, then the dedicated educators who populate those schools will feel defensive and resentful of how our society demeans them. They rightly feel besieged from all directions. At the same time, these conscientious individuals are working extremely hard and accomplishing much more than the high school was designed to do.

Fortunately, if we realize that the high school is obsolete, we can validate what our high school educators are doing and work collaboratively with them to design a new high school that works for all of our youth. If we are to be successful in educating all students in a new age, we need to redesign our high school for the new age.

Left Behind by Incremental Improvements

In November 2005, the social policy research organization MDRC conducted a conference in San Diego focused on connecting education research to practice. As the conference wore on, it became increasingly obvious that the researchers who were presenting their reports were acting on the premise that the high school was broken and could be fixed. In that vein, they stressed the need to see incremental improvements in achievement test scores as schools were implementing changes.

As I pondered this often-repeated guidance, I thought about the origins of high schools a century earlier. I thought, "Here I am in San Diego. When high schools were designed, if I had traveled from the East Coast to this conference, it would certainly have taken a weeklong train ride to get here." But, I got here in hours because I could take a plane.

I realized that if we focused on incremental improvements, we would be doing what the railroad companies had done a century before. They might have made the trip incrementally better by increasing passenger comfort. They might have improved fuel efficiency or improved scheduling so that the trains ran on time. However, by focusing on those incremental improvements, the railroad companies lost sight of the changing needs of U.S. society. No matter how many incremental improvements they made, they would never be able to get that train to fly. The railroad companies saw the world from the perspective of a provider of a service that was assumed to be irreplaceable. As a result, they lost sight of the changing needs of their customers—not unlike educators today.

Fortunately, during that same time, the Wright brothers were experimenting with flight. If their investors had required that they measure progress against the same indicators that the railroad companies did, then the airplane would have been relegated to the trash heap. Eventually the airplane could in fact be assessed by the same measures as the railroad—and could far surpass what was possible in long-distance train travel. In fact, the airlines were eventually able to carry passengers farther and faster than anyone had imagined possible. Had we continued to invest only in strategies that showed incremental improvement using the traditional measures of success, we would still be traveling by rail.

—*Joseph DiMartino*

◆ ◆

Open to Possibilities

In many ways, the situation we face in our high schools is similar to the situation the railroad companies faced. Railroad officials kept their mission narrow. They thought of themselves as being in the railroad business, not in the travel business. They lost sight of what was possible. Rather than investing in the Wright brothers' efforts, they chose to ignore the possibilities. Those who see the high school as broken are displaying the same behavior. Their vision is blinded by their preconceived notions of what a high school should be. They continue to see the high school as an institution with tracks. However, we know that the tracks existing in our schools cannot reach the new mandate of educating all our youth to high standards.

The last panel of the San Diego conference included practitioners who had demonstrated success in changing high schools. They all spoke of how important personalization was to their efforts. Ray Daniels, the recently retired superintendent of the Kansas City School District in Kansas, which has received tremendous accolades for its astounding turnaround of its high schools, cautioned that achievement test data for the district's high schools were stubbornly flat for five years after implementation of major change initiatives. It was year six before the steady upturn in assessment results started to show, and that remarkable increase continued for the next five years. He cautioned that to be successful in the short term, school practitioners needed to pick their indicators carefully. They needed to identify appropriate leading indicators that would eventually show the desired outcomes—and to acknowledge that achievement test scores were more likely lagging or weak indicators.

High Schools That Fly

The stories in this chapter exemplify the confounding mix of complexity and seeming simplicity that our high school educators face. Students and educators are stuck in an institution that remains remarkably durable despite credible evidence that it is unable to meet the new demands of our society. This rigidity has frustrated everyone involved in high schools. Fortunately, many educators have been conscientiously pursuing a new path, resulting in the emergence of high schools that are radically different from current institutions. Simply stated, *the new vision of high school is schooling that puts students at the center of their learning.* All further changes proceed from that idea.

Perhaps this vision seems too simple, but it is so profoundly different from the current reality that it holds the potential to resolve our current educational dilemma. Although the image of the new high school is simply stated, the change has been extremely difficult to achieve, because it begins to transform all the facets of high schools that stabilize a large organization.

Fortunately, emerging evidence shows the viability of this new vision. A number of schools, districts, states, and national organizations have recognized that student learning should be the center of high school systems. A growing body of evidence points to personalizing high schools as the only hope for the future of our secondary schooling. In MDRC's recently released report on the efficacy of three high school reform models, Janet Quint (2006) identifies benefits from personalization in each model and finds correlating improvements in some leading indicators of success, including higher attendance rates, greater persistence in school, and lower dropout rates.

Personalized high schools engage students in using knowledge to plan and develop their own pathways through school, depending on their talents, interests, aspirations, and general standards for graduation. This book, therefore, explores promising practices that are emerging in high schools across the United States: guiding personalized learning, personal learning plans, personalized teaching, community-based learning, personalized assessment, and rethinking the Carnegie unit. As we discuss these themes, we identify successful practices and offer advice gleaned from initiatives proven in the field.

2

GUIDING PERSONALIZED LEARNING

THE VALUE OF ADVISORIES

"With so much work to be collected, how do you keep track of it all?" asked an associate superintendent from an urban district in Rhode Island. The young woman speaking to the group was surprised at the question because the answer seemed so obvious to her. She and another senior from Francis W. Parker Charter Essential School in Devens, Massachusetts, had just completed a presentation on Parker's portfolio requirement at a small conference on performance assessments convened by a department within Brown University. Both students had been articulate in discussing the evidence of a rigorous education as they presented their graduation portfolios. The student looked at the questioner in amazement and said, "We have an advisor who works with us."

The young lady had just shared a research paper from her huge arts and humanities binder. She had explained how this paper was one of two dozen artifacts included in her portfolio. She also had explained how the topic of the research was of deep concern to her and how it connected to standards for performance. She had included in her presentation her proposal for the arts and humanities project, with several initial drafts, each building on the previous one and leading to the final paper that was deemed good enough to be included in her arts and humanities portfolio. She then had gone through a similar process to explain a piece of work included in the second huge binder, this one for math, science, and technology.

The small group of adults in the room included a few teachers but consisted mostly of high school principals, district-level administrators, and higher education representatives from the area. After each of the two presentations, the adults in the room peppered the students with questions. "Do you have options on what goes into your portfolio?" "How do you know when an artifact is good enough?" "Have you ever thrown out an artifact?" It was at that point that the assistant superintendent, obviously impressed, had asked how this student kept track of it all. The young woman had looked bemused. After all of the grilling, this was clearly a softball question. She had worked closely with her advisor to create a portfolio that would meet school expectations.

She explained that during her advisory period, her teacher/advisor made sure she was following her personal learning plan, doing all of the work required for her graduation portfolio as well as other school work and advisory group projects. In addition to this support, her advisor had helped her decide on projects to pursue, including identifying a community service project to complete. Her advisor helped when she needed it. What had surprised her was that the adults in the room didn't know the value of advisory, which was so basic and obvious to her. Her reaction to the question made it clear that she couldn't comprehend how adults at high levels in the educational system didn't know that advisories were a central and important part of her education.

—*Joseph DiMartino*

◆ ◆

Lessons from Exemplary Schools

Between 2000 and 2006, the Secondary School Redesign program at Brown University conducted an annual high school showcase that included presentations from 20 exemplary high schools from around the United States. The schools presenting had been identified as outstanding by an outside third party. They included Blue Ribbon Schools, New American High Schools, New Urban High Schools, and Breakthrough

High Schools, as identified by the U.S. Department of Education and the National Association of Secondary School Principals. The purpose of the showcase was to support practitioners from good schools in their goal to become great schools by gathering and illustrating successful personalization strategies.

A team of teachers and administrators from a high school in Providence, Rhode Island, had listened to the presentations of all 20 of the schools at one showcase and had become energized by what they saw and learned. As each team member recounted the program at the schools that he or she had observed, it became apparent that some trends existed across all the sites. The showcase schools demonstrated some common themes, including the following:

- Offering an advisory program with a clear purpose.
- Looping students so they saw the same teachers over more than one year (for many of the schools, the looping took place in advisory).
- Planning weekly professional development opportunities for the entire school staff.
- Strongly expressing the understanding that they hadn't reached their goals yet and still had much to improve.

These themes drove the approach to high school redesign adopted by the Brown University Secondary School Redesign initiative. Two of the themes—advisories and looping—can be addressed through the implementation of an appropriate advisory program. The other two themes reflect a school that relies on dialogue for professional development and understands that resting on one's laurels is bound to result in moving backward. Both looping and community dialogue can be strengthened through an effective advisory program.

The Purpose of Advisories

Across the country, many outstanding high schools have been implementing programs to support personalization for students and adults in the school. These programs are labeled in several ways: advisory, mentor-mentee relationships, families, advisor-advisee, or teacher advocacy programs. For the sake of simplicity, we use the term "advisories" to describe all of these initiatives, which feature small groups of students (usually fewer than 20) that meet regularly with a single adult who acts as a guide or advocate for each student.

Successful advisories share a few more traits. They (1) have a stated purpose that everyone in the building knows and accepts as the clear goal for the program, (2) are organized to meet that purpose, (3) have written content guidance for the routines and activities that take place within an advisory period, (4) have a defined method of assessing the advisory program for improving the advisory system, and (5) have school leaders who embrace the concept of advisory so it is a continuously improving system that supports positive outcomes for students.

The purpose of advisories can run the gamut from simply being a place where students can have a conversation with an adult in the room to the place where personal learning plans and portfolios of student work are developed and assessed. The goal could even be to build school community and break down problematic cliques that exist in the school. Whatever the goal or purpose is, it has to be the result of a planned and concerted effort to engage the school community in meaningful conversation on what's missing in their school and how an advisory program could address the school's needs.

For any high school faculty, clarifying the purpose of advisories is an important first step. Beginning to design a program structure without a shared sense of what the advisory is meant to accomplish is a step toward confusion and hard feelings. The following list (Clarke, 2003a) is a collection of some possible purposes that a high school might use to focus its advisory program.

- To increase student motivation
- To guide course selection
- To help students imagine their future
- To connect families to student learning
- To celebrate student achievement
- To connect each student with a caring adult
- To relate student work to standards

- To explore noncurricular options
- To support identity formation
- To initiate lifelong learning
- To increase self-awareness
- To emphasize applications of knowledge
- To gather a best work portfolio
- To banish anonymity from school life
- To clarify graduation requirements
- To plan a path after high school
- To prepare for college application
- To define a personal pathway
- To promote reflection and reevaluation
- To improve basic skills
- To explore career choices
- To develop personal talents
- To extend community involvement
- To evaluate content acquisition
- To legitimize nonschool achievements
- To prepare for college applications

Clearly a list this long would frustrate most advisors. If a faculty can select four to six purposes that they can develop together across the grade levels, they can define a manageable task that produces a coherent program.

Successful advisories are organized to meet the school's explicit advisory goals. For example, if the advisory has a clear academic purpose, the decision about who should be an advisor is decidedly different from who would be able to advise a group that's focused on community building within the school. When the purpose is academic, advisors might be limited to teachers and administrators. However, when the purpose is building community through advisories, virtually every adult in the building is capable of being a good advisor. Likewise, when and where and for how long and how often the sessions occur is dependent on the school's stated purpose. The school's purpose or mission should drive the organization and content of the advisory period and should be consistent with an overall personalization plan for the school.

Aligned with school goals, a successful advisory program develops a curriculum for advisors to use in creating daily activities, units, or student performances. This curriculum must include sample routines and lesson plans for advisors to draw from. In many schools, faculty members are free to create their own activities that are consistent with a broad theme. In yet other schools, students are encouraged to take an active role in creating content for the advisory program. Teacher- and student-designed activities can enlarge the school's repertoire of advisory options. Again, it is important that the school create content that is consistent with the stated purpose and that can be accomplished through the organizational plan designed to meet that purpose.

Both formal and informal assessment processes are an integral part of successful advisory programs. Assessment can be informal, such as scheduling reflection time for advisors to collectively review how things are going and help one another improve on what happens within their advisories. Advisors can schedule reflection time in their advisories for the same purpose. Assessment can be more formal, including a survey of advisors, advisees, and parents to gain feedback and ensure continuous improvement of the program. Regardless of how formal or informal the feedback loop is, the critical aspect of assessment is that the school use suggestions gained from this feedback to make meaningful improvements to the system.

As with any endeavor to change the culture of the school, strong leadership is required to implement and maintain an advisory program in the school. Eliminating the anonymity that currently pervades the culture of our schools is challenging to students and faculty alike. Ensuring that each student is known well by at least one adult and knows well one adult in the building is not what most teachers expected when they chose high school teaching as a career. Leaders are faced with guiding an effort that will require staff members (and students) to rethink their roles in a way that may challenge their core beliefs. Without effective leadership, any advisory program is doomed from the start.

Illustrations of Successful Advisories

Illustrating successful advisories in several U.S. high schools can show how different schools have approached the core tasks of developing new advisory programs.

Setting Advisory Goals

The staff members at Granger High School in Granger, Washington, have embraced the following five advisory goals:

- Every student will be well known, both personally and academically, by at least one adult staff member.
- Every student will be pushed to increase his or her reading level and math level.
- Every student will be challenged to meet rigorous academic standards in an appropriate educational program.
- Every student will be provided with opportunities to experience the benefits of community membership and to develop and practice leadership.
- Every student will be prepared for whatever he or she chooses to do after graduation, with a strong transcript, a career pathway, a plan, and a portfolio.

Wyandotte High School in Kansas City, Kansas, established the following goals for its Family Advocacy Program (its advisory program):

- For students to have someone in their corner, day after day, no matter what challenges present themselves.
- For teachers to build a strong and lasting relationship that will cheer on successful students and put struggling students back on track.
- For parents to have an assurance that their child is known and watched over by someone in the school who genuinely cares.

At Parker Charter Essential School in Devens, Massachusetts, the purposes of the advisory program include the following:

- Academic advising: The advisory is a place to develop personal learning plans (PLPs), to monitor student progress in general and toward specific goals, to discuss teachers' assessments with students and parents, and to build on the habits of learning.
- Community service: The advisory is a place to practice being an active member of the broader community by designing and implementing community service projects.
- Community conversations: The advisory is a vehicle for school-wide conversations about community issues and about being a community member.
- Recreation: The advisory is a place to have fun and to learn about group process and dynamics.

All three of these advisory programs have similar purposes, but each also has a special focus: academic skills, student advocacy, or community participation. The differences reflect different community expectations. The career pathway, plan, and portfolio are requirements in Washington State, so it is appropriate to the advisory program at Granger High, but not in Kansas City. The PLP is a central aspect of the curriculum at Parker, so advisory has become the most appropriate place to monitor that progress. Parker staff members see advisory as a place to promote community service, but the other schools do not have that focus.

Early in the process of developing the Family Advocacy Program in Kansas City schools, Wyandotte High School, which was in the first cohort, sent a team of 20 teachers and administrators to a summer institute on the power of advisories in Providence, Rhode Island. During that time, team members agreed on the purpose and plan, including a process for gaining feedback from the entire adult community to strengthen their purpose (National Education Association, n.d.). Agreement on the purpose for advisory requires lengthy conversations with all involved. Ideally, students are included in the conversation so that an advisory's ultimate purpose is informed by all groups within the school community.

Organizing an Advisory Program

The three high schools just described defined very different purposes for their advisories, based on three very different school communities. Consequently, each school organized an advisory program specifically to support its unique and fitting purpose.

Granger High School organized its advisory program by heterogeneously grouping students within grade levels—with a teacher designated to guide those students for their entire stay at the school. That basic structure supports the primary purpose of Granger's program—making every student known well by at least one adult. The advisories at Granger meet four times a week for 30 minutes at the end of the school day. That schedule provides ample time for developing relationships that facilitate accomplishing the advisory program's remaining four goals.

The Kansas City high schools, including Wyandotte, have an 18-to-1 ratio of students to advocates. All teachers must serve as advocates, and other classified staff may also serve as advocates. As at Granger, advisory groups stay together for the entire four years of high school. In the Family Advocacy Program, advocates work to improve learning for each student. They meet with their group of students at least once a week, and contact each student's family at least once a month. Two family conferences are held with students and their families each school year—one each semester. To monitor academic and behavioral problems for each advisee, advocates have an opportunity to meet and consult regularly with core teachers.

At Parker, with a strong academic purpose that is connected to classroom instruction, the advisory is organized so that each student has an advisor who is also his or her classroom teacher. Students are placed in advisories each year using the following set of criteria:

• A student is placed in an advisory based on age, with secondary consideration given to the academic division of the student.
• A student is placed in an advisory in which the advisor is also one of the student's teachers.
• A student may request to be placed in a particular advisory.

- A teacher may request placement of a student in his or her advisory.
- Advisory groups should be gender-balanced and should be representative of Parker's diversity.

All full-time teachers serve as advisors. Part-time teachers are asked to coadvise or to serve as substitutes.

At Parker, advisories meet approximately three hours each week, with morning connection (8:30–8:45), afternoon reflections (3:20–3:30), and extended time on Wednesdays (12:30–1:30). Advisory serves as one of the primary avenues through which students' voices are heard and through which students have ownership of the school. Most advisories have to share a room, so it is expected that those sharing space will establish shared norms. Each advisory elects one member to the Community Congress and to the school's Justice Committee. Juniors and seniors serve as peer mentors to 7th and 8th graders in advisory. Each advisory has a parent volunteer who serves as the advisory parent representative. The role of this parent is to support the advisor in achieving the four purposes of the school's advisory. The advisory program throughout the school is supported by an advisory coordinator.

Activities in an Advisory

To address school goals in Kansas City high schools, each advisor is expected to do the following:

- Get to know students individually and as a group.
- Develop positive relationships with the students.
- Help students develop positive relationships and a sense of community among themselves.
- Provide students with the supports and skills they may need to be successful in school and adult life.
- Keep a confidential file that faculty members can check to see how best to support a student.

An advisory program guide supports advocates by providing relevant activities, exercises, discussion topics, and guidelines.

At Granger High School, advisors who help students enroll in classes each semester are also expected to know if a student is struggling in any particular class. Every semester, each student organizes a student-led conference for other students, teachers, and parents or guardians. Advisors help their students prepare for the conference. At the conference, students present what they are learning, how they are progressing on their personalized education plan, what their grades are, what their reading levels are, and what interventions, if any, are needed. Prior to the conferences, advisors touch base with other teachers to make sure that everyone—students, parents, and teachers—is on the same page with the same information.

At Parker Essential School, some curricular elements, such as PLPs, are common to all advisories. Otherwise, advisors are expected to create a curriculum that aligns with the four stated purposes of the advisory program. The advisory coordinator provides a common set of protocols from which advisors can draw their lessons.

Assessing an Advisory System

Parker provides a variety of vehicles for assessing all aspects of the advisory system, including assessing students, advisors, advisory groups, and the advisory system as a whole. Students are assessed by progress on their PLPs and on advisory checklists mailed to students' homes four times per year. Advisory groups are also assessed at the completion of their community service project by submitting a community service plan and evidence of completion. Advisors are assessed periodically by observation and by occasional feedback from students and parents through surveys designed for that purpose. The advisory system is assessed as part of a larger whole-school community survey that includes questions about the effectiveness of advisory. Figures 2.1, 2.2, 2.3, and 2.4 show examples of these feedback and survey forms.

FIGURE 2.1

Student Assessment of Advisories at Parker Essential School

Name: _____   Advisory Reflection

	Never	Rarely	Sometimes	Mostly	Always
I connect in advisory.	1	2	3	4	5
I enjoy coming to advisory.	1	2	3	4	5
I feel left out in advisory.	1	2	3	4	5
I feel like I had input into our Wednesday activities.	1	2	3	4	5
I feel comfortable in advisory.	1	2	3	4	5

Name the people you feel closest to in advisory.

Who is someone you would like to know better?

How do you feel about advisory in general? How could we, as a group, make it better?

What was your favorite Wednesday activity?

How could we make our Wednesdays better (more organized, more varied)?

How can I, as your advisor, better support you through the year?

Final thoughts:

Source: Used by permission of Debbie Osofsky, Advisory Coordinator, Francis W. Parker Charter Essential School.

FIGURE 2.2

How Are We Doing as an Advisory?

Please rate the following statements on a scale of 1 to 5, with 1 being Strongly Disagree and 5 being Strongly Agree.

	Strongly Disagree				Strongly Agree
I look forward to advisory time every day and am eager to participate in advisory activities.	1	2	3	4	5
I feel other advisory members actively participate in advisory on a regular basis.	1	2	3	4	5
I feel comfortable speaking in advisory.	1	2	3	4	5
I think others listen respectfully when I speak in advisory.	1	2	3	4	5
I listen respectfully to others when they connect.	1	2	3	4	5
The members of our advisory support one another in reaching their PLP goals.	1	2	3	4	5
Our advisory is planning/performing valuable community service.	1	2	3	4	5
Our advisory has planned some fun activities and we are reflecting on our development as a group.	1	2	3	4	5
Overall, everyone contributes to our advisory goals.	1	2	3	4	5
I contribute to our advisory goals.	1	2	3	4	5

Comments…

Source: Used by permission of Debbie Osofsky, Advisory Coordinator, Francis W. Parker Charter Essential School.

FIGURE 2.3

Francis W. Parker Charter Essential School Parent/Guardian Advisory Feedback Form

Dear Parent/Guardian,

Please take a moment to answer the questions below about your child's advisor. Your input is valuable to us as we reflect on our practice as advisors. You do not need to note your child's name, but please indicate the name of the advisor about whom you are giving feedback. Thank you.

Advisor_____ Date _____

Question	Yes	No	Comment
1. Do you feel you can contact your child's advisor with any questions or concerns you have?			
2. Do you feel your child's advisor understands your child and responds well to his/her needs?			
3. Do you feel your child's advisor has kept you informed of your child's academic progress?			
4. Do you feel your child's advisor has kept you informed of other issues related to your child's school experience?			
5. Have you been invited to participate in the PLP process with your child by his/her advisor?			
6. Do you feel comfortable sharing information about your child that may impact his/her school experience with his/her advisor?			
7. Do you feel your child has developed a positive and caring relationship with his/her advisor?			
8. Do you feel your child's advisor is serving as his/her advocate in the school?			
9. Do you feel your child's advisor sufficiently monitors his/her academic progress and advises your child and you accordingly?			
10. Do you feel your child's advisor satisfactorily guides the advisory group toward meeting the stated purposes of the advisory program?			
11. Other comments?			

Source: Used by permission of Debbie Osofsky, Advisory Coordinator, Francis W. Parker Essential School.

FIGURE 2.4

Student Assessment of Advisors

Dear Advisee,

Please take the time to thoughtfully complete this Advisor Assessment. We take your opinions very seriously, and as we discuss our professional practice, these assessments will play a significant role. Please note: This is not about whether you like or dislike your advisor. It is about the quality of facilitation you are experiencing. Please take this seriously. Answer the questions carefully and honestly.

Directions: Please assess your advisor's work in each category below. Please explain your assessment in the space provided.

Advisor's name_____ Date _____

For each question, choose the answer that best characterizes your advisor's work in the area. Choose one of these answers: JB (Just Beginning), A(Approaching), M(Meeting), or E(Exceeding).

• Knowledge of advisory purpose: Is your advisor clear about the purposes of advisory? Does he/she seek to help the group meet these purposes?
　　JB　　　　　A　　　　　　　M　　　　　　　　E
　　Please explain:

• Advising style: Does your advisor use a variety of methods to facilitate the advisory group? Does his/her style motivate and engage advisees?
　　JB　　　　　A　　　　　　　M　　　　　　　　E
　　Please explain:

• Ability to organize advisory content: Do you like the activities you do in advisory? Do you learn from them? Do you see their connection to the advisory purposes?
　　JB　　　　　A　　　　　　　M　　　　　　　　E
　　Please explain:

• Classroom management skills: Does your advisor maintain an appropriate advisory environment? Does he/she help the advisory resolve conflict and stay on task?
　　JB　　　　　A　　　　　　　M　　　　　　　　E
　　Please explain:

- Relationships with advisees: Does your advisor listen to students? Does he/she treat advisees with care, compassion, and respect? Does he/she try to understand advisees?

   JB   A   M   E

   Please explain:

- Serve as your advocate: Does your advisor serve as your advocate? Does he/she help you resolve difficult situations, access various resources, and refer you to others when appropriate?

   JB   A   M   E

   Please explain:

- Academic advising: Does your advisor help you through the PLP process? Does he/she monitor your progress in academic classes and toward your PLP goals? Does he/she create opportunities for reflection and celebration?

   JB   A   M   E

   Please explain:

- Individual meetings: Does your advisor meet with you individually during the year to maintain communication and to address academic and social concerns as needed?

   JB   A   M   E

   Please explain:

- Connection to home: Does your advisor have contact with your home? Does he/she help to answer questions, explain decisions, and celebrate your successes with your parent/guardian?

   JB   A   M   E

   Please explain:

- How would you assess your own performance, attitude, and behavior in this advisory?

   JB   A   M   E

Source: Used by permission of Debbie Osofsky, Advisory Coordinator, Francis W. Parker Charter Essential School.

At Granger High School, the method of assessing the effectiveness of the advisory program is based on two indicators of student success. One is the percentage of students who have a parent attend the student-led conference. The other indicator reflects how students are performing academically, primarily based on achievement scores on the state assessment tests. Both indicators showed a clear pattern of improvement once the advisory program was put in place. In the first year of advisor-supported student-led conferences—in 2000—about 20 percent of students had parental participation in the conferences, which was twice the percentage of parents who attended parent–teacher conferences during the previous year. In the second year, the percentage of parent participation in student-led conferences grew to 100 percent and stayed at 100 percent for four years. This measure provided a clear indication that the school and the parents were committed to supporting student learning.

During that period, the achievement test scores also showed dramatic gains. The percentage of students meeting state standards reflected improvement in the basic skills portion of state achievement tests (WASL). Most students were still arriving at Granger High achieving at well below grade level. The cohort of middle school students tested in 2001 had passing rates of less than 15 percent in reading and less than 5 percent in math when they took the 7th grade WASL, and yet their 10th grade WASL scores at Granger in 2004 were substantially higher. Those 2004 scores, shown in Figure 2.5, represent dramatic increases when compared with the school's 10th grade WASL scores three years earlier. The graduation rate also rose substantially, as shown in Figure 2.6.

FIGURE 2.5
Comparison of 10th Grade WASL Scores at Granger

Subject	2001	2004	2007
Reading	20%	47%	76%
Math	4%	31%	31%
Writing	8%	52%	66%

These percentages represent the number of students meeting standards on the WASL.

FIGURE 2.6
Granger High School Graduation Rates

Year	Percentage of Students Graduating
2000	58.3%
2001	69.0%
2002	85.2%
2007	95.0%

Perhaps the most remarkable evidence of success is the drop in the school's crime rate. Granger High's reported crime rate in 1999 topped all the high schools in Yakima Valley, but by 2003 it was the lowest of all the Valley's high schools.

Granger High faculty and staff are accustomed to looking through a variety of student data to focus improvement on priorities of the school and its advisory program. For example, concern for the number of students receiving failing grades soon resulted in the implementation of a no-failing rule. Now any student who falls below a C grade in course work is required to get extra help until the grade improves. The advisors are the key communication link to this program, keeping students, teachers, and especially parents informed about student progress.

Methods of assessing the performance of the students, advisors, and the complete advisory program are critical to the sustainability of the initiative. The Kansas City schools advocates are observed, assessed, and coached in their role by family advocacy staff and principals during walk-throughs. Students also provide feedback on the efficacy of the system during periodic roundtable discussions of the advocates.

Leadership

Richard Esparza, the principal of Granger High, has an approach to leadership for advisories that is based on his firm belief that high schools must do the right thing for their students. He realizes that to reach all students, high schools need to know all students.

Parker has designated an advisory coordinator who provides support and plans and conducts professional development so the advisors can be more effective. Two to three full faculty meetings per year and summer planning time are devoted to advisory. Much of this time is dedicated to tuning the PLP process to ensure that PLPs continue to improve student outcomes and guide the teaching and learning at the school.

Advising may not come easily to some high school teachers—or to schools where other traditions prevail. Advisories require teachers to get to know each student within a group of 12 to 20 students. Teachers realize that getting to know each student can be difficult, particularly if a student is not happy with the high school experience. Because content acquisition is not the paramount purpose for advisories, teachers often fear that they lack the skills they need to work closely with students. "That's for the guidance office," they may say. High school teachers may also be uncomfortable with the open format of the advising session, which can be governed as much by fluid student interest as by an established sequence of plans.

High school teachers often choose their profession because they have two major interests, their academic disciplines and their commitment to student learning. Elementary teachers often choose younger students because they love kids. College teachers tend to choose teaching because they love their disciplines—and were quite good at them. High school teachers have both interests but tend to feel most confident working with an established tradition of facts, concepts, procedures, and processes.

At the same time, high school teachers spend a good deal of time after school and elsewhere talking with students who get excited about the subject itself. Typically, they work with those students in the same role as that of an advisor. In the classroom, their commitment can be profoundly influential among many students. Most adults have little difficulty identifying the high school teachers who made a difference in their lives. Asked why those teachers were influential, high school graduates seldom refer to disciplinary knowledge—although they do see excitement about the subject as powerful. More often, they refer to a sense of humor as the main ingredient of success. They remember whether a teacher cared about how they did in school. They think of times a teacher may have stopped in the hall or cafeteria to talk with them. They remember interacting with a teacher informally, talking about the news, sports, entertainment—or life itself. In those settings, teachers show that they do have the skills (if not the self-assuredness) they need to be an effective advisor.

Students also contribute a great deal to the difficulty of working effectively in an advisory. Many students try to avoid adult contact because it undercuts their own sense of authority. Adolescents are famous for their ability to alienate themselves from the adult world. As 14- to 19-year-olds, they have escaped the confines that oppressed them earlier at home and in school. As adults themselves, most will slowly develop confidence in their contacts with older people. As high school students, however, they seem determined to tear down the structures that adults have created on their behalf.

What does it take to proclaim freedom? Edgy music? Rude or rebellious language? A hat? Baggy pants? Dark glasses? Dope? Pregnancy? A fast car? Whatever it takes, high school students are out to declare ownership of their lives. The remarkable thing is that most high school students do succeed in transforming the uproar of their high school years into the behaviors and responsible roles of adults in the community— people they tried so hard to avoid in their youth.

Schools beginning to develop advisory programs do not face a uniform group of teachers any more than they serve a uniform set of young people. Consequently, programs for faculty need to be multifaceted. Formal professional development workshops and courses may play an important role in creating a common language and setting up structures for a schoolwide program. Colleges and universities may be willing to create school-based courses or longer programs for a school aiming to establish an advisory program.

Although professional conferences are frequently available, most of the training needed to develop local capacity for change can be found within the school itself. Some teachers pride themselves on their relationships with students. They can help form a steering group to organize a long-term process of development. Other teachers are curious about life in other schools; they can be encouraged to travel to schools with strong reputations for advising. By far, the most important effect of any road trip will occur in the car or van as a team is driving to and from a distant event.

Simply engaging teachers in teams that take on the various challenges that accompany development can have an effect. Creating a program guide, writing optional lesson plans, interviewing parents, surfing the Internet, or researching scheduling options can activate teachers with different interests. Allocating time to mutual education within a faculty is essential. By engaging all the faculty, school leaders can remove the adoption barrier that goes up whenever one group of teachers is inside the development circle while another group remains outside.

To avoid resistance (and subterfuge or sabotage) among students, it is essential that they become part of the design process. They know what is possible and desirable. As much as teachers, students need the time to work and rework a new idea in their heads. Most important, students need to have the experience of working closely with adults to solve problems and make something happen. That process is the essence of advising.

If teachers begin to talk about advising in the lounge or halls while students are also talking in the cafeteria, heat begins to rise within the school community, building energy and focus. Working together creates momentum. Simultaneous momentum in several essential areas requires the support of a reliable structure and coordination. Advising is not the kind of activity that can be dropped on students and faculty from the top. It grows most energetically when teachers and students tend to its growth together.

3

PERSONAL LEARNING PLANS

PERSONALIZED LEARNING AT THE MET

I met Joe Claprood at a conference on competency-based assessment in New Hampshire. I sat next to Joe at a session, waiting to hear Steve Jubb, the executive director of the Bay Area Coalition of Equitable Schools, describe how experiential learning was developing in some high schools in the San Francisco area. At that time, Joe was a junior at the Metropolitan Career and Technical High School in Providence, Rhode Island, called the Met. The Met is an innovative high school that has taken experiential learning to an extreme rarely matched by any other high school in the country. Students at the Met get all their learning through internships and projects that are guided by personal learning plans (PLPs). The results for Met students have been documented elsewhere, and they are positive. Typically, all seniors at the Met are accepted at a college (Steinberg, 2001).

Joe explained to me that he had started his freshman year at the Met and had liked it well enough, but many of his friends were at his neighborhood high school. So, after a successful freshman year, he chose to transfer back to the neighborhood high school. It didn't take Joe long to realize that moving from class to class every 45 minutes and having virtually no say in his education wasn't for him. So, he returned to the Met to finish his high school experience. After Steve Jubb completed his presentation, Joe took over a fairly large portion of the session, describing his personal experiences to the 50 or so people in the room.

I was so impressed by Joe's ability to explain the kind of personalized learning he had designed at the Met that I would later ask the school's administrators how Joe was doing. At another conference, I listened while Eliot Washor, one of the founders of the Met, explained how the senior year at the Met was different from earlier years. Eliot explained that the senior experience continued to be guided by each student's PLP, but the senior project was much more rigorous and demanding than the four projects a year students had completed in their first three years. To describe the special challenges of the senior year, Eliot used a compelling illustration—Joe Claprood's senior project.

Joe had mentioned in advisory that his dad had fought in the Vietnam War but would never discuss his wartime experiences. As a result, Joe incorporated into his PLP an interest in learning more about Vietnam. He also decided to do his senior project on the Vietnam War, but in a dramatically powerful way. He did substantial research on the war and created a credible report—and set the goal of going to Vietnam with his father. His PLP goals included criteria to measure this project against real-world standards.

Joe conducted various fund-raising activities. And he and his father actually did make that trip, where the two of them discussed his wartime experience—at the point of origin. Ultimately, as the final demonstration of meeting his personal goals, Joe and his dad made presentations at American Legion Posts and other veterans' organizations across Rhode Island, providing their different perspectives on the war and the visit. As shown in the national media and during the 2000 campaign for U.S. president, Joe met with John McCain, Vietnam War hero and senator from Arizona, and personally discussed the experiences of war and captivity.

Joe Claprood graduated from the Met in 2000 and was the first in his family to attend college. At Rhode Island College, he made the dean's list numerous times, and he graduated in 2004. Joe then returned to the Met as an advisor—seeking to help others in the way that he was helped.

—*Joseph DiMartino*

◆ ◆

Engineering Their Own Learning

Most students enter 9th grade without a compelling vision for their own learning. Many have learned passivity as a way to avoid responsibility. Many have learned to comply with adult demands because compliance is easy and risk-free, particularly if they regularly earn high grades. Some want to hide, avoiding adult authority and the risk of public embarrassment. Others have begun full-scale rebellion, committed to rocking the structures that adults have erected to contain their reckless energy. A few are simply furious, outraged that they have left a history of failure and frustration in middle school only to face four more years of the same. They can compensate for their perceived abuse by earning a reputation for heroic resistance. They can fight hard, take drugs, show up drunk— and eventually drive fast or make a baby. The problem with the kind of compensatory behavior that high school students use to demonstrate their freedom, individuality, and personal strength is that those behaviors gradually erode their freedom, individuality, and personal strength. The extent of that erosion can be seen in the 30 percent of 9th graders who, across the United States, do not graduate with their high school classes.

To learn at all, students have to engage themselves in learning. Despite the effort of teachers, learning is something that students have to do for themselves, rather than something that others can do for them—or to them. That simple rationale forms the foundation for PLPs, sometimes called personal plans for progress. A personal learning plan is a document created by a student and a caring adult to guide the student through the high school experience on a self-designed pathway toward active participation in work and college. Unlike four-year course plans, PLPs are dynamic planning tools, designed to change as the student discovers opportunities that reflect a sharpening sense of direction. PLPs usually include self-awareness activities and goal setting. Increasingly, a PLP also includes extracurricular activities, such as arts, work, travel, internships, and personal projects—as well as courses—that fit a student's interests, aspirations, and talents, and clarify choices for roles in the adult world. Students with PLPs often exhibit their PLP progress on a regular basis each year. The student and an advisor change the PLP as the student learns and gains clarity about work and college.

Students can begin their PLPs in 7th grade, 9th grade, or even later—but there is little chance the PLP will look the same as the first draft after several semesters of learning, each of which helps the student refine goals and identify learning opportunities that fit those evolving goals.

The basic difference between personalized learning and individualized learning lies in control. In personalized learning, control lies largely with the student; in individualized learning, the control lies with adults. Unlike most individualized education plans (IEPs), a PLP is based on a student's personal talents, interests, and aspirations rather than deficiencies. An IEP is often based on test scores and other diagnostics and aims to raise the student's level of performance, but a PLP is based on dreams, questions, or personal concerns that a student can revise after any new experience, clarifying his or her sense of direction. IEPs identify remedial services that can help students meet appropriate expectations; PLPs help students identify the kind of learning they need to do to fulfill their own evolving hopes. If IEPs aim to reduce weakness, PLPs aim to extend the positive momentum of each individual.

Because they have different purposes, PLPs and IEPs can be used in tandem. (In states such as Vermont, PLPs first entered high school learning through special education.) Both IEPs and PLPs prove helpful because they do not assume that all individuals are the same. Both assume that students learn most effectively when the high school experience responds to their unique skills and understanding, opening pathways to adult commitments.

A whole population of students pursuing their own idiosyncratic PLPs puts some pressure to adapt on virtually all the elements of a high school system. Still, each part of the conventional system has its own purpose to which PLPs must also respond. Students following PLPs may use their work experience, athletics, travel, or creative work to fulfill their plans, but they still need to work within a common schedule and meet graduation requirements. They may design a focused project in the community, but their advisor may ask them to include some parts of algebra, writing, earth science, or global history to meet school standards. In high schools with established core courses or distribution requirements, PLP students cannot be exempt, but they may choose virtually all their electives to answer personal questions from their PLPs.

PLPs can often help students meet the particular standards associated with specific content areas, but they certainly help them accumulate evidence that they have met more global 21st century standards—such as communication, problem solving, and social responsibility. PLPs are an important aspect of student-centered high school learning because students produce a higher quality of work when they know that advisors, friends, teachers, and family will help measure their success against common standards.

Student engagement in high school depends a great deal on shifting control from adults to students, often in staged increments from grades 9 to 12. PLPs train students to take control of their own lives. Student engagement also depends on the respect that students earn from teachers and peers. Successful PLP inquiry earns respect, not because each student achieves high scores on a common test, but because each student presents progress against common standards by producing a unique response to personal challenges. Fully developed PLPs ask students to express their knowledge and opinions in their own voices, earning praise and recognition for their unique performances. PLPs force students to see the connections between their own efforts and their own accomplishments. Shifting control from teachers to students requires careful attention to student readiness, faculty preparation, curriculum flexibility, and community understanding.

Levels of Intensity

It is easy to contrast personalized learning fully organized by PLPs with subject-centered learning fully organized by course sequences and core requirements, but most high schools seek a middle ground. Conventional curricula and PLP explorations coexist in many high school settings. In some subject-based high schools, student PLPs are listed as credit-bearing courses, with grades assigned by the advisor and collected by the guidance office. Other high schools schedule meetings with a faculty advisor just once a week or for a few minutes each day—simply to plan course selection, spot students in need of services, or discuss progress in student PLPs. Other high schools use PLP formats to help students organize student-led conferences, at which they explain their performance to parents and family.

To make PLPs more manageable, some high schools relegate PLP development to special programs, such as alternative programs, 9th grade academies, or academies in a small school initiative, an approach that integrates team teaching with ongoing PLP advising. In a few high schools such as the Met, each student's PLP constitutes a personal curriculum, planned with an advisor, parents, and peers, to propel each student into college and adult roles that fit their personal pathways. When PLPs organize most of a high school program, that school offers a personalized program of learning—leading each student to fulfill personal goals while also meeting standards established by the high school. The range of student control in PLP development is represented by the scale in Figure 3.1, from homeroom to student-directed high school learning.

FIGURE 3.1
A Continuum of PLP Adoption in High Schools

In Subject-Based Curriculum				*In PLP-Based Curriculum*
Homeroom and guidance	Weekly PLP advising	PLPs in student-led conferences	PLPs in special programs	PLPs as curriculum guides
5–8 minutes	15–40 minutes	5 hours/quarter	40 minutes/day	whole semester/year

Which use of a PLP format serves to engage all students in learning? Homeroom may have been designed to connect each student with a caring adult, but most homeroom activity seems to be administrative. Weekly PLP meetings give students a chance to reflect on their week, but planning requires more time with a teacher who understands the advising role. Preparing students to lead a scheduled conference forces them to assess progress against standards and also against the expectations that friends, teachers, and family have of their work. When the PLP work is organized by a team of teachers with responsibility for a large proportion of a student's schedule, the student can begin to see connections between course work and personal goals, and the team can devise assignments that differentiate among students with differing views of themselves in the future. Clearly, a PLP approach that shapes the whole student experience seems to engage the largest number of students. Personalized high schools such as the Met in Providence, University Heights High School in New York, and New Technology High School in Napa, California, regularly report college acceptance rates that approach 100 percent each year (Steinberg, 2001; Washor, 2003).

PLPs help each student learn to use knowledge to manage his or her own life in the adult world and to participate in our democracy so his or her voice blends with those of others. Developing a PLP with a caring adult who follows progress and guides choices over several years can show each student how knowledge works in his or her area of interest—how knowledge really makes a difference in what is possible for any person to achieve. Devising a plan and testing it in course assignments or community internships shows students how a well-developed plan can lead to adaptation or abandonment of that plan—and the selection of a better path. As adults, we earn money, respect, self-confidence, and a chosen lifestyle not by replicating the success of others but by building a novel approach to success and meeting an unmet social need. Students need knowledge to succeed. They also need practice accompanied by guidance from helpful adults. PLPs can be designed to lead students through a cyclical process of assessing the current situation, as shown in Figure 3.2. They learn to ask questions, seek answers, and use information to design new solutions—the stuff of responsible adult work in any setting.

FIGURE 3.2
A Process for Personal Learning Plans

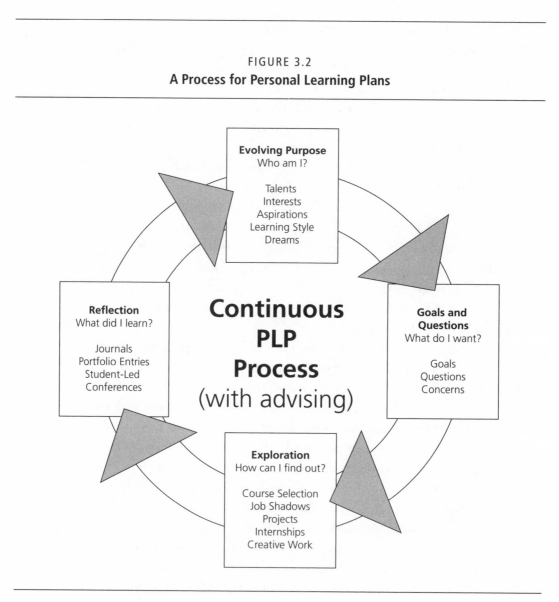

The Shape of Personal Learning Plans

In 2004, the National Association of Secondary School Principals (NASSP) made personal learning plans a central component of its recommendations for high school renewal in *Breaking Ranks II*. NASSP's representation of the plans, called personal plans for progress, emphasizes the need for constant revision and stable standards for performance:

> Each student will have a Personal Plan for Progress that will be reviewed often to ensure that the high school takes individual needs into consideration and to allow students, within reasonable parameters, to design their own methods for learning in an effort to meet high standards. (NASSP, *Breaking Ranks II*, 2004, p. 18)

As NASSP stated, the planning process should aim to help students design their own methods for learning and revise those plans to make transitions from successful high school experiences into adult life. Those two aims remain at the center of most high school PLPs.

In general, the PLP process follows four basic steps, which are stages in a recursive and self-correcting cycle of inquiry. (1) Inquiry usually starts with the current perceptions of each student: Who am I? What's my purpose? (2) Students can convert their primitive statements of purpose to goals or questions for exploration. (3) The explorations themselves usually contain courses—core, elective, and college courses—as well as experiences in the school and surrounding community. As they develop PLP projects, students collect evidence of their discoveries. (4) To promote adaptation of the original purpose and to generate new goals, a student can present findings to a class, an advisor, or a supportive group consisting of parents, teachers, and friends—and use the discussion to refine the PLP.

Mount Desert Island High School in Maine uses only three focusing questions to guide PLP development: Who am I? How am I doing? Where am I going? This approach lays the groundwork for reflection within an advising process fully consistent with the school's statement of purpose, which is to "guide students as they acquire the knowledge and skills necessary to become responsible, self-directed learners, and healthy, productive citizens" (Mount Desert Island High School, n.d.). An overview of the PLP approach (shown in Figure 3.3) can be found on the school's Web site, with links to more detailed information.

FIGURE 3.3
PLPs at Mount Desert Island High School

What Are Personal Learning Plans (PLPs)?
Organized around three simple questions—Who am I? How am I doing? Where am I going?—PLPs address the unique strengths, interests, and priorities of students with the guidance and support of their advisor, teachers, and families. PLPs are dynamic; ideally they guide all students' learning and educational plans. While many aspects of the PLP are documented on paper, most important is the relationship that exists among students, advisors, and parents/guardians. Student-led conferences provide a formal opportunity for the student, advisor, and parent/ guardian to meet to discuss the student's learning and the Personal Learning Plan.

Personal Learning Plans at MDIHS are organized around the following questions (click on any of the questions below to see the four-year overview):
• Who am I?
• How am I doing?
• Where am I going?

What are the benefits of Personal Learning Plans?
• PLPs give students a stake in their education.
• PLPs give teachers a vehicle for getting to know their students and families on a more personal level.
• PLPs give the students' families increased opportunities to be involved in their children's education.
• PLPs provide a valuable learning experience that teaches students to set goals, evaluate their work, and take greater responsibility for their own learning.
• PLPs allow for the recognition of students' interests and achievements beyond a purely subject-based focus.

What are the big ideas behind Personal Learning Plans?
Students learn best when
• They have goals to guide their learning.
• They understand clearly what they are trying to learn and what is expected of them.
• They are fully involved in making decisions about their learning, about what they need to do next, and who can give them help if they need it.
• They are given feedback about the quality of their work and what they can do to make it better.

MDIHS is grateful for the work teachers at the following schools have done on Personal Learning Plans: Montpelier High School, Poland Regional High School, Bonny Eagle High School.

Reprinted with permission from Mount Desert Island High School (2005).

At Mount Abraham Union High School in Bristol, Vermont, PLP planning has become a feature of middle school houses, new freshman teams, and a collection of connected courses in the Futures Academy, a PLP course organized by teachers in science and social studies to help students explore career options related to various disciplines. Students can enroll in Futures Academy courses sequentially or scatter them throughout their program. They can also enroll in internships, senior projects, or independent studies, electives that they take to extend their career explorations. Student PLP explorations vary widely and sometimes dramatically as students refine their goals and locate new resources in the community.

The range of PLP and related explorations at Mount Abraham Union High School has begun to stretch the conception of what is possible for high school students to do. One student designed and successfully flew a model 1937 stunt airplane, crashed it—then went on to study engineering in college. Another started a small company designing handbags from brightly colored cloth—then went on to study clothing design in design school. Another designed and built a cabin with her father, became an adequate carpenter—then went on to college much more confident than she had been. Another designed and built a composting system at the town dump, made a little money—then joined the army.

As achievements such as these enter general discussion around the school, other students begin to think about their own talents, their own questions, and projects they might take on to complement their course work. Teachers begin to include project-based learning in their classes. Community members begin to see that students at the high school can bring courage, new ideas, and bright hopes to old challenges.

Guiding Questions for Crafting PLPs

In the Futures Academy at Mount Abraham, four questions guide PLP development: Who am I? What do I want? How can I find out? What did I learn? The following sections explore those questions in more detail.

Evolving Purpose: Who Am I?

PLP processes are organized to help students redefine themselves throughout the high school experience. Guided PLP exploration promotes evolution of answers to the question "Who am I?" Answers based on specific achievements prove powerful in helping students proclaim an identity that can open new choices. "I make pottery." "I presented a study showing that noxious bacteria thrive in our storm drains." "I love meeting new people in retail sales." When individual accomplishments, preferences, styles, histories, or hopes are seen as the essence of self, the combinations are infinite in number. Each student becomes unique. Their talents make each of them special. Recognizing that weaknesses limit the range of choice, they can learn to use their talents to overcome them. The first phase of PLP development often opens with the question of identity, but in fact the whole cycle is a process of self-realization. Students ask personal questions. They accomplish new tasks. They reflect on their work and emerge with an expanded sense of their abilities.

The question "Who am I?" defies easy answers, for high school students as well as older people. No single answer will suffice for any of us, because time and experience change our sense of self. In a high school setting, questions of identity are often defined by groups: "I am a cheerleader." "I am an honors student." "I am college bound." "I travel to the VoTec center." "I am on the absent list." Although identity based on groups defined by the school—or even by peers—simplifies the process of managing a large school, group-based identities do little to help high school students direct their own lives. Group membership is the stuff of cliques, tracked classes, status assignments, and prejudice. In most regards, membership in a class or group lies beyond individual control, at least in daily interactions. Most high school students are not famous for complex understandings of themselves beyond their group affiliations. Many, however, are interested, particularly when the question can help them earn independence and respect.

All four phases of PLP development organize the longer-term investigation of self-identity, but many resources have been developed to help students work with their advisor or advisory group to recognize their distinctive characteristics. Figure 3.4 lists and describes some of these tools, which include different formats for self-study. Many more choices can be found with a Google search on "learning styles," "interest inventories," "career inventories," "personality profiles," or "personal writing." Most profiles and inventories are proprietary, but some are free. The use of these tools should be closely tied to a clear purpose, leading toward steps that clarify the written results. The tools should help students ask questions or set goals for inquiry into the meaning of the results.

FIGURE 3.4

Methods of Clarifying Student Self-Awareness

Method	Description
Surveys and Inventories:	
David Kolb's Learning Style Inventory	Comparative view of learning preferences: concrete vs. abstract, reflective vs. active.
Bernice McCarthy's 4MAT	Similar to Kolb, with methods for using strengths to improve weaknesses.
Dunn and Dunn Learning Style Profile	Questionnaire including personal characteristics and workplace preferences.
Myers-Briggs Type Indicator	Personality profile in four dimensions: extraversion/introversion, sensate/intuitive, thinking/feeling, and judging/perceiving.
Strong Interest Inventory	Questionnaire connecting personal interests to possible career options.
Writing Processes:	
Free Writing	Brainstorming on a focusing question related to personal history, dreams, fears, or goals.
Learning Logs	Journals written over time to make sense of learning or experience.
Personal Narratives	Formal essays on critical events in the development of personal direction.
Interview Write-Ups	Articles written from interviews with family and friends on talents, interests, and future.
Inquiry Processes:	
MAPS (Making Action Plans)	Concept maps focused on self-description, personal history, dreams, fears—and needs or goals.
Personal Collage	Photos and images reflecting personal attributes or a desired future.
PowerPoint Presentations	Crisply worded media events featuring beliefs, career aspirations, and personal talents or accomplishments, including PLP field studies.

By far, the most important tool in clarifying purpose lies in what the student has already done to answer the same question. Discovery and disappointment both generate new questions to answer. In PLP development, self-awareness is insufficient in itself. Self-awareness should lead to questions about the future and what it will take to get there.

Goals and Questions: What Do I Want?

Teenagers and young adults are not often noted for understanding why they do the things they do. For clarification, they often look toward their peers, who may appear headed in a clear direction—whether off to college or to buy a handgun. For many, the idea of setting a personal goal seems foreign and potentially frustrating. They might respond in the following ways: How can I know anything about the future? How can I gain control of my life? What if I change my mind? High school students tend to focus on short-term goals: Can I get the car? Will Margie be there? Can I avoid embarrassment? At the beginning of PLP development, instead of setting formal goals, students often explore their wants: What do I want? Teachers and advisors can ask the same question again and again, allowing students to revise and narrow their answers after periods of experience, thought, and understanding.

Moving students toward easy answers is not the goal of the PLP advisor at Mount Abraham's Futures Academy. Rather, the advisor uses focusing questions to generate follow-up questions, each of which drives the student deeper into knowledge from the subject areas or the surrounding human scene. The experience of one Mount Abraham student over a full year may illustrate how questions evolve through the PLP process. As the student set out to discover what he wanted, he began to wonder whether tapping birch trees for sap and syrup might be more lucrative than tapping maples. His PLP advisor, community mentor, shop teacher, and members of the community all helped him develop follow-up questions much more specific than the first: How can I measure profit? Can I explain the yield of each tree over the season? What size pan will I need to boil down the syrup I have predicted? The sequence of follow-up questions and the conclusions he came to are shown in Figure 3.5.

An initial estimate of costs led him to write a formal proposal for external funding from the Boy Scouts of America. Exploring the Internet, consulting with birch syrup makers in Alaska, building a copper boiling pan in shop class, boiling down the sap, and assessing the result prepared him to answer his own question—in the negative. After three nights of boiling sap back in the birch woods, he produced a bit less

FIGURE 3.5

Sequence of Questions During Birch Syrup Exploration

Main PLP Question and Reflection	Following Questions	Information	Answer
What do I want?	Fix cars?	Shadow a car repair shop	Too many skilled people
	Will diesel pay better?	Visit to diesel shop	Too much math
	Make maple syrup?	One season with a neighbor making sugar	I don't have my own trees
	Why not tap birch trees?	Write e-mail to Alaskan birch tappers	Two Alaskan families do all right
	How many trees to make a gallon of syrup?	Calculations (Estimation)	Twenty might do it
	How much money per gallon?	Calculations (Estimation)	Estimate of income
	What does it cost to start?	Contact distributors (First rough budget)	I'll get donations; too expensive
	Can I sell this idea to a foundation?	Written proposal in six drafts (Writing)	Proposal writing is slow business
	Can I design and build most of the equipment?	Project in metal shop (Geometry and Fabrication)	Fine (small) boiling pan in copper
	Can I find enough birch trees?	Survey with community mentor (Science)	Identify three different birch species
	Will they produce?	Tap and boil with friends in abandoned sugar house	Less than 1 gallon
What do I want?			An easier job with reliable income

than one gallon of syrup. Although he struck birch syrup from his hopes for the future, he saw that he had become what would pass for an expert in the remarkably small field of birch syrup production.

Does a failed birch syrup enterprise represent failure? Hardly. The student involved in tapping trees and boiling sap began his questioning without a sure idea of what he might want and what it might take to get there. In the Futures Academy, he had explored diesel mechanics, hydraulics, and small engine repair before focusing on birch trees. In each phase of questioning, he organized resources from the high school and surrounding community that would help him find answers. Birch syrup pushed him to a new level of sophistication. In proposal writing, sap-pan construction, and business development, he faced a series of barriers— each of which helped him see what he wanted and what he could do for himself. He wrote and submitted his proposal to a national audience. Between his sophomore and junior years, he became a young adult who could manage his way through a difficult enterprise. Was that what he set out to find? No. However, the result was far more important.

Exploration: How Can I Find Out?

The search for meaningful answers may surely be the most rewarding part of a PLP inquiry, but it is also the most difficult for teachers and advisors to manage. In part, high schools were designed in the early 20th century to protect adolescents from exploitation by adults beyond the school. Responding to family worries, high schools have since operated in loco parentis, temporarily replacing parent authority with school-based monitoring. The walls of the school contain a separate world, governed by separate rules and inhabited by a group of people the same age. The unintended effect of high school walls is that they prevent contact between young adults and experienced adults in the community who can help them find a path. The unintended effect of in loco parentis supervision may be that it prevents students from learning to take responsibility for their own actions.

Preparing students to assume responsibility for serious inquiry into a field of interest puts a high school on a tightrope between maximum safety in the classroom and maximum engagement in the surrounding community. Parent involvement in PLP development spreads the risk and responsibility, while enriching the pool of knowledge that students can explore.

When PLP exploration is limited by existing school policy restrictions, many students produce results that are one-dimensional, uninspired, or pro forma—lacking the vigor of hands-on research. Exploration beyond school walls entails much more risk—both for the school and for each student—and multidimensional products infused with passion may not be the uniform result. Four support structures make the difference between a successful high-risk exploration and a diffuse effort that loses students, parents, and other teachers to anxiety:

- *Detailed guidance* that shows students and others how to take the necessary steps to complete their exploration.
- *Close contact with a universe of community mentors* who take responsibility for supporting the student's exploration.
- A *close relationship and regular contact with a teacher/advisor* who works with 10 to 14 students on different kinds of exploration.
- *Parent involvement*, at least at student-led conferences and special events, but also in deeper roles promoting mutual learning.

Helping students become independent learners relies on a variable stretch of time during which some students need daily support and others take charge right away. Focusing professional time on small groups has become a reason for making PLPs part of a credit-bearing course.

High schools that have taken community exploration guided by advisors to impressive lengths rely on full-semester community-based learning experiences over four years. The Met high school in Providence, Rhode Island, is surely one of those. All students at the Met go out to their internship sites two full days a week. Their advisors monitor the sites but also prepare PLP assignments that engage the core subject areas. At the end of each semester, students explain their internships to a roundtable of parents, friends, teachers, and mentors, who then recommend new goals for the next version of the PLP.

One sophomore with a Hispanic background found herself in the local hospital aiding elderly Hispanics with their basic comforts. She soon noticed, however, that her patients could not understand what the doctors and nurses were saying in English. She became their interpreter in writing and speaking, using terminology far more complex than the stuff of Biology 1. Her experience with elderly patients became the basis of a more focused PLP for the next semester, which involved the following:

- More writing in Spanish

- More writing in English
- Learning medical terminology and basic physiology
- Making a deeper assessment of the cultural divides
- Exploring metrics in medicine

In other words, the community-based learning helped her focus her PLP on math, science, social studies, English, and foreign language. She needed to become capable in all five areas to help her clients and prepare for college. To illustrate the kind of challenge that PLP students may undertake, Figure 3.6 lists a sample of community sites where other students at the Met have begun testing their vision for the future.

At the early stages of PLP exploration, teacher/advisors and mentors need a great deal of patience while their students practice the basics of self-directed learning and face the fearful turmoil that occurs when young people begin to push themselves into the adult world. Students, in their unique way, do not start at the same place or make progress at the same rate. In one semester at the Futures Academy at Mount Abraham Union High School, for example:

- A student explored three separate areas—finance, business, and the travel industry—before he narrowed his inquiry to study-abroad programs.
- A student spent a full month writing and revising a letter of introduction to a social service agency (achieving perfection in letter writing formats), before she had her interview and claimed an internship position.
- A student working with an individualized education program, or IEP, completed a full-semester internship in a recording studio before coming to believe there was no future in that area.

Like the adults they want to emulate, students can take painful hits in the world of work, community service, or arts that can jolt their confidence and test their commitment. That raw experience is what PLP explorations are meant to provide. Those risks are also why advisors, mentors, detailed guidance, and tightly scheduled steps are essential to the success of a PLP program.

FIGURE 3.6
A Sample of Met Internship Sites

The Alfred Lima School
The Bailey School
The Big Picture Company
Child Center Inc.
Children's Shelter of Blackstone Valley
Christopher Foster Glassworks
City Garden Flower
Classical High School
Club Neopulsi Creations
Cohen's Fashion Optical
Common Cause
Community Prep School
Concept Link LTD
Connie and Nicki's Restaurant
Cozy Corner Child Care Center
CVS Highlander Charter School
Daily Bread
DARE
Diane Hiller Photography
Earthenwares
East Providence Boys & Girls Club
East Providence Police Department
Easter Seals Cornerstone Preschool
ECentricSites
Emmaus Youth Center
Erik Bright Ceramics
Ernie Potters Carpentry
Esek Hopkins School
Estelle Hero—Designer
FCCE/URI
Federal Hill House
Festival Ballet
The Flynn School
Focus Childcare
Fortes Elementary School
14 Sloop Providence
Friendship Head Start
Full Circle Gallery
Gregg's Restaurant
Haffenreffer Museum of Anthropology
Hamilton House
Hasbro Children's Hospital Gift Shop
Headshots Photography D.B.A. B.A.Z.
Historical Preservation and Heritage
Hi-Tone Records
Hoffman Animal Hospital

Iglesia Metodista Primitiva
Innovative Network Solutions
Intercity Contemporary Arts
International Yacht Restoration School
J. Juan & Associates, LLC
Jack and Jill on the Hill
Jobs for Ocean State Graduates
John Hope
John Hope Day Care
Joseph Cornwall—Architect
Knight Memorial Library
LaSalle Bakery
Lifespan Corporation
Looking Glass Theater
Luke's Music
MAP
Martin Luther King School
Mashantucket Pequot Museum
MeKenna Performance Products
The Met
Minority Investment Development
    Corporation
Moses Brown School
Muchi Muchi
Napa Valley Grille
Navy Recruiting Station
Needlenose Productions
New Technology Computer
Newport Collaborative Architects Inc.
Nicholas A. Mattiello—Attorney
North Providence Assembly of God
Oil and Grease on Wheels
Paul Cuffee School
Perishable Theater
Perry Middle School
Pilgrim Enterprise
Pinegate Farms
Planned Parenthood
Pleasant View School
Precision Saw & Mower Service Inc.
Project New Urban Arts
Providence Art Club
Providence City Hall
Providence Mayor's Office
Providence Police Mounted Command
Providence Tae Kwon Do

The Public Archaeology Lab Inc.
Quisqueya in Action Inc.
RE/MAX 1st Choice
RI Children's Crusade
RI Department of Education
RI Department of Labor and Training
RI Foundation
RI Hospital
RI Hospital Print Shop
RI School for the Deaf
RI Select Commission on Race and Police
    Community Relations
RI Small Business Development Center
RI Tech
RI Youth Guidance
Roger Williams Middle School
Roger Williams Park Zoo
Rolling Thunder Light & Sound
Rumford Pet Center
Ryan Walquist—Artist
Sandra Feinstein Gamm Theatre
Save the Bay
Scott Lapham—Photographer
Sew Biz
Skippy White's
Solo Insurance
Standard Times
State of RI School to Career Office
Step by Step Dance Studio
Tavares Pediatric Center
Team Computer
Tec Direct Inc.
T.F. Green Airport
Tockwatten Home
Tolman Interactive
Trinity Encore
Trinity Repertory Company
Urban Bankers of RI
Urban League of RI
Visiting Nurse Association
Warwick Animal Hospital
Warwick Police Department
Waterview Villa
Wavelight Design Inc.
Women and Infants Hospital

Source: From the Met School Portfolio, 2001–2002. https://www.bigpicture.org/publications/metportfolios.htm. Used by permission of Elliot Washor.

Reflection: What Did I Learn?

In PLP development, reflection has two purposes related to assessment. The first is to help students understand how what they have learned affects the plans they have developed. The second purpose is to assess student work against the standards a high school has developed to understand student progress. The first motive for assessment is formative, aiming to support the changes a student has made and will make toward personal goals. The second is more formal, providing signals to students, teachers, and others that further progress toward the standard is desired.

Although rubrics support both aims in most schools, student PLP assessment rarely aims for the objectivity offered by standardized tests and even course grades. For this reason, PLPs do not generate the kind of comparative data that produce class ranks and honors status. Instead, PLP assessment creates a record of change across the high school years, a compilation that employers and college admissions staff often view as having face validity.

In many high schools, self-assessment is often the first step in a weekly, monthly, or semester review of personal progress, with student goals in view. Figure 3.7 is the form developed by the Futures Academy at Mount Abraham Union High School to guide students every two weeks. Students review their goals, mark the progress they have made through projects and internships, then meet with their advisor to troubleshoot their plans. Less regularly, Futures Academy students present an important product from their work to their advisory group, receiving feedback from friends, teachers, and community mentors. At the end of each semester, students present their complete PLPs to a whole class, with parents and mentors often present and teachers using the course rubric to assign grades. Figure 3.7 shows a two-week planning guide that Futures Academy teachers use to conference with students and keep them on track.

The Futures Academy also includes assessment criteria in the program packet to help students, advisors, and mentors keep educational purposes in view as students work through their field experiences and prepare their roundtable presentations. Figure 3.8 shows an example of the problem-solving assessment. The criteria help teachers formally evaluate

FIGURE 3.7
Two-Week Learning Contract from Mount Abraham Futures Academy

Your Name:_____ Primary Advisor:_____ Cluster/Focus:_____

Contact Person:_____ Contact's phone:_____ e-mail:_____

Learning Contract

(Remember to keep your eye on the prize.) (8 points) Goal:

	Comfort/Risk/ Danger	Goal	Identify Problem or Solution Made	Student Grade	Teacher Grade
Feb. 8				/4	/4
Feb. 10				/4	/4
Feb. 14 **ROUND TABLE**					
Feb. 16				/4	/4
March 1				/4	/4
March 3				/4	/4
March 7				/4	/4
March 9 **Advisory RT**				/4	/4

Round Table Date: February 14

(5 points) At the end of this contract, what is your evidence of learning and how will you demonstrate it? Remember that you need to link what you have been doing for these two weeks with what you are demonstrating in Round Table. This will be a connection grade at Round Table.

Source: Used by permission of Kristen B. Farrell, Mount Abraham Union High School Futures Academy.

student progress, yet they play an equally important role in establishing a common lexicon for students, advisors, and evaluators to use in speaking with each other. The assessment criteria also promote reflection. In roundtables, students review their experience to select events that require problem solving. With other students, they look for components from the assessment document and evaluate their effectiveness. No student experience in problem solving may reflect all the criteria, but the use of the terms helps students see problem solving as steps they can manage for themselves. In roundtable discussions, student-led conferences, and portfolio presentations, the document provides a common framework for all participants to consider as they look at projects that otherwise do not resemble each other at all. This assessment framework serves students throughout their work in the academy.

Managing the PLP Process

Because PLPs have to accommodate so much variability, their daily management belongs with a small group of teachers and students who can set up common routines. Creating guidelines, timetables, and group activities helps foster a climate of mutual support among students. In seeking and obtaining field placements, creating products and artifacts, and setting up materials for presentation, students can manage their own work, supported by caring adults. The school itself should create a common framework for PLP development, keeping the vast population of PLP students, advisors, and community mentors moving along in tandem. The school should also support smaller teams as they set up their own processes. As Figure 3.9 shows, Bonny Eagle High School in Maine has connected its PLP process to existing systems, such as grading, as well as schoolwide schedules. The growth of specific procedures occurs largely through the work of students and teachers.

Electronic PLP Liberation

When members of the Coalition of Essential Schools began experimenting with PLPs and PLP portfolios, one result was unmanageable mounds

FIGURE 3.8
Futures Academy Problem-Solving Assessment

Criteria	Cite Evidence Here
Made observations of the situation.	
Discussed and listed probable causes and effects of the situation.	
Made connections between this situation and others that are similar.	
Looked for patterns within the situation and/or between this situation and others that are similar.	
Generated questions to help trigger ideas.	
Generated hypotheses and discussed possible solutions.	
Used process of elimination to help work toward a solution.	
Got ideas and information from other sources (friends, teachers, books, etc.).	
Tested different approaches to solving the problem.	
Made adjustments along the way.	
Used drawings or objects to model or act out the problem and/or used numbers or formulas to help solve the problem.	
Considered and investigated more than one solution to the problem.	

Source: Used by permission of Kristen B. Farrell, Mount Abraham Union High School Futures Academy.

FIGURE 3.9
Personal Learning Plans at Bonny Eagle High School

"We must all learn to view the secondary school years as a purposeful transition to a productive future, not as an end in itself." —*Promising Futures,* p. 50

Most Frequently Asked Questions About the Personal Learning Plan (PLP)

1. What is the purpose of a PLP?

The purpose of a PLP is to fulfill Core Principal #6 of the *Promising Futures* document. "Every student employs a personal learning plan to target individual as well as common learning goals and to specify learning activities that will lead to the attainment of those goals."

2. What are the goals of a PLP?

- Identify student's learning style.
- Create strategies for each student to meet goals and standards that align with the Maine Learning Results (MLR).
- Identify student's academic strengths by documenting samples of best work.
- Develop future plans by establishing academic, career, personal, social, and cocurricular goals.
- Review and additions are continuous.
- Record academic and cocurricular honors and awards.
- Examine and document personal interests and abilities, as well as community involvement and volunteer work.

3. When do students work on their PLP and where is their PLP kept?

Students compile their work during Extended Home Base periods conducted eight times a year. Students have the same Home Base teacher for their entire high school career. Home Base teachers store the student PLP in their classroom.

4. What is the goal of the PLP after high school?

The goal is for the student to continue to add to his or her PLP and develop academic and personal goals. The student would have a "main" PLP to showcase his or her post-secondary work and accomplishments. The PLP can be utilized as a tool or template for a professional portfolio.

5. How and when is the PLP credit awarded?

Credit is awarded upon the "certification" of a completed PLP. Student transcripts will reflect a grade of "P," Pass. In order for a PLP to be certified, the following signatures are required: student, Home Base teacher, parent/guardian, and principal.

6. How will incomplete PLPs be managed?

New, transfer students, or challenged students will attend PLP make-up sessions each spring.

Source: Used by permission of Robert A. Strong, Principal, Bonny Eagle High School.

of paper. Although PLPs are meant to be flexible, paper-based PLPs proved very hard to adapt. Growth in student learning generates new piles of physical documentation, punishing the most enterprising students most severely. Now, technology has begun to solve the problem with electronic PLPs and portfolios. A Google search for "personal learning plans" will yield a vast array of electronic formats for PLP development, some of which are commercial but many of which come from the United Kingdom for free. Some electronic formats include lesson plans for advisors. Electronic PLPs do entail an additional phase of learning for students and teachers. Like earlier technological innovations, however, electronic PLPs can move into a school culture if they are used widely to collect student work. Mount Abraham Union High School has used several pilot programs to create an ePLP portfolio that includes grades from a standard transcript. Student work is linked to the courses or PLP experience that generated it. Mount Abraham electronic PLP portfolios have proven influential in getting borderline applicants into both highly selective and less selective colleges.

The electronic portfolio index in Figure 3.10 shows how Mount Abraham students in Futures Academy and the 9th grade programs create an indexing page that links to items on the student's portfolio Web site. The list on the left shows how the student is meeting the state's content area standards, represented by grades. The four categories at the top of the index represent Vermont's higher-order skills: communication, problem solving, personal development, and social responsibility. Any academic course can help students produce artifacts showing competence in these four areas. In addition, PLP explorations, independent studies, dual-enrollment papers, community service projects, sports, work-based learning, and other cocurricular activities can produce evidence for the portfolio. Each number in the matrix represents a specific standard, and the electronic version of this document would link to the artifact on the student's Web site that shows evidence of meeting that standard. This document, with active links and artifacts, may be found on the school's Web site at http://www.mtabe.k12.vt.us/Portfolios/laferrari/standards_based_transcript.htm. A student could attach this type of portfolio and transcript to an online job or college application.

FIGURE 3.10

Electronic Portfolio and Transcript at Mount Abraham Union High School

FIELDS OF KNOWLEDGE				VITAL RESULTS Notes: Vital Results identified here are documented in the accompanying electronic portfolio. Please click on the Vital Result number to go to the sample of student work demonstrating success at meeting that standard.			
Junior Year (2001–2002)							
		Credits	Grade	Communication	Problem Solving	Personal Development	Social Responsibility
Arts, Language, Literature	Yearbook A	.5	A+				
	American Studies A	.5	B+	1.16			
History, Social Science	American Studies A	.5	B	1.16			
Science, Math, Technology	Integrated Math	.5	C+		2.2		
	Math Lab						
	Chemistry A	.7	B-				
Other Courses	Enterprise.com	.5	A+	1.15		3.15	
	Internship			1.5, 1.6, 1.13	2.6, 2.7, 2.8, 2.9, 2.13	3.10, 3.11, 3.13, 3.14, 3.15, 3.16	4.1, 4.3
	SUMMARY	3.2	3.3				
Applied Learning	Reporter/writer Eagle Gazette			1.5, 1.6, 1.9, 1.13			
	PASTA meeting attended				2.1, 2.4		4.1, 4.2
	Job interview analysis			1.15		3.15	
	Speaker: Statewide teachers conference: Vital Results			1.13, 1.14, 1.15, 1.21	2.8		4.1
	Socially Conscious Youth						4.1
Class Rank	**Cumulative GPA 3.32**					**Other**	
Distinctions: Lana was invited to speak at a statewide conference for educators called "Achieving the Vital Results." She demonstrated the standards-based transcript and portfolio project which she volunteered to help develop.							
ADVISOR COMMENTS: Lana has an uncanny ability to communicate, as is clearly documented in her portfolio.							

Source: Reprinted from *Standards-Based Transcript: Mount Abraham Union High School* (http://www.mtabe.k12.vt.us/Portfolios/laferrari/standards_based_transcript.htm). Used by permission of Kristen B. Farrell, Mount Abraham Union High School Futures Academy.

Challenges to PLP Development

PLPs are certainly not a widespread method for personalizing learning and engaging all high school students. Except in states such as Maine, Oregon, Washington, Rhode Island, and Colorado, which require their development, they have become a feature mostly in smaller charter schools and educationally progressive high schools. Their greatest value is also their most formidable limitation: PLPs destabilize most of the conventions used to organize large high schools. They refocus school priorities on individual needs rather than subject-area knowledge, undermine the practice of comparison that schools use to rank and track students, and threaten the conventional roles that teachers and school administrators use to organize their own lives.

Because PLP development destabilizes most existing systems, incremental adoption of personal learning plans is prohibitively difficult. Most schools that have successfully used PLPs to engage students have had to start from the beginning, creating house systems or smaller learning communities where program redesign is feasible. Other schools have chosen to create pilot programs on a smaller scale—in academies, grade-level teams, or alternative programs, for example—hoping to expand the PLP process into the whole school.

Pilot PLP programs can work quite well in the context where they are first grown and still not make the transition into wider use. When a school begins PLP development in the 9th grade, for example, it may eat up all the resources in faculty time and funding that it needs to move to the 10th grade. If a pilot freshman program does successfully make the transition to the 10th grade, it may draw in and, in effect, use up all the faculty members who are willing to try PLP development, dividing the faculty in half—into believers and nonbelievers. Particularly when early PLP developers receive external funding, special travel opportunities, new leadership responsibilities, and lots of public acclaim, early nonbelievers may feel disenfranchised and devalued. Conflict may follow. Some nonbelievers may form a loose coalition to fight PLP development in favor of business as usual. The following section identifies notable areas of resistance to PLP development, along with strategies that high schools have used to modify existing systems so PLP development can begin.

Student Readiness for Personalized Learning

Resistance: Inexperience with self-direction. High school students have had little experience assessing their own strengths, setting goals, carrying out field explorations, or marking their own progress. For many, the prospect of developing a PLP is frightening because it opens them up to criticism from peers, teachers, and outside mentors. Students are accustomed to making others responsible for their learning.

Adaptive Strategy: Smaller learning communities. Reducing the size of the context in which students build and test their plans allows students to gain confidence without fear of ridicule. Developing goals and questions over four years (or longer), guided by a few trusted adults, allows students to begin with simple explorations, change their minds, and slowly discover more promising pathways for their explorations.

Faculty Readiness for Advisory Roles

Resistance: Inexperience with student-led learning. Many teachers base their professional identities on the subjects they teach. Most have designed their courses so they can focus closely on teaching groups of 20 to 40 students, often in patterns set by textbooks. They view covering the content as a legitimate purpose and responding to students as questionable. Most important, few teachers have experience with advising. The argument "I wasn't trained as a counselor" can be a way of resisting the expansion of their roles.

Adaptive Strategy: Team teaching and professional learning communities. Working with a small team of peers, teachers can design and test PLP approaches that are consistent with their skills and aims. Team meetings can become the center of shared experimentation, and team success can bolster their pride. A professional learning community throughout the school can expand the range of teacher exploration, promote further sharing of ideas, and make PLP development a schoolwide initiative.

Graduation Requirements

Resistance: Core course requirements can limit options. Requirements for courses in core areas, often with a set pattern of distribution, can constrain the time students and advisors have for broad exploration beyond the school. Clearly, PLP development depends on the availability of real choices in school and the community. When core courses are required each year, elective teachers may face dwindling enrollments in their courses and may have to take on a large load of advisees to fill their time. Elective teachers find it hard to teach outside their areas.

Adaptive Strategy: Credit toward graduation for outside learning. Outside exploration can gain more respect in the school community when independent studies, internships, service learning projects, creative work, and work-based learning offer credit toward graduation. Groups of students with similar interests become part of the teaching load. Schools can create a cross-disciplinary department to avoid having to wedge PLP courses into the subject area framework. Elective teachers can design student-directed learning within their own interest areas.

Scheduling Patterns

Resistance: Changing without adding. Faculty loads and required courses often dictate the school schedule. Scheduling PLP advisories with sufficient time can encroach on the length of classes or the number of course sections that can be offered. PLP credits offered through electives can threaten teachers of elective courses. Adding a new dedicated time for advising can put the squeeze on the time and staffing available for Advanced Placement and special departmental courses. Shifting student demand can change faculty assignments each year.

Adaptive Strategy: Integrating PLP advising. In a smaller school arrangement—an academy, house system, or grade-level teaching teams—PLP advising can become part of the team's work. Block scheduling creates opportunities for PLP development. An integrated curriculum can also create flexible time for PLP advising. Integrating PLP development with academic courses allows teacher/advisors to watch their students closely, making modifications or providing academic support as the need arises.

System Coherence

Resistance: Misalignment. High school systems are locked together, not only within the school, but also with earlier grades and college or work after graduation. Subject area proficiency has become the basis for high school tracks and college admissions. Not all colleges have changed admissions policies to allow PLP portfolio applications or the submission of cross-disciplinary student work. PLP credits may not be seen as equivalent to subject-based credits.

Adaptive Strategy: Reconnecting to Employers and Colleges. A student's experience in a subject-based elementary curriculum can become part of the first PLP question, Who am I? A project-based PLP portfolio can be a very persuasive part of a job interview, showing how problems are solved using information. Many colleges now allow PLP portfolio submissions— preferring e-portfolios to bulky notebooks. PLP portfolios sharpen the focus of interviews for admissions and increase student confidence.

Vision

Resistance: Cross-purposes. Parents, teachers, administrators, and students have become accustomed to high schools that protect adolescents from outside forces, apply uniform standards to behavior, see learning mainly as knowledge acquisition, and focus on the basics. In any community, people understand and accept personalized learning at different rates. Many may feel that PLP development will not lead to acceptance in a competitive college or university. Others want tighter teacher control over adolescents, *in loco parentis*.

Adaptive Strategy: Celebration. By far, the most powerful method of public engagement is not to proselytize but to focus attention on student work. Parents, friends, and mentors who know what a student has done are likely to show up for student-led conferences, semester roundtables, and yearly PLP presentations and exhibitions. Seeing the diversity in presentations, they grow to understand PLPs. The public presence of students in local businesses and agencies spreads the concept of PLPs around the community. Newspaper articles on student projects can help.

PLPs at the Center of Personalized Learning

Personalized learning plans certainly can disrupt the ongoing practices of a conventional high school. The tendency to destabilize a very large number of adolescents and young adults can be a reason to start school personalization from some other vantage point. Alternatively, high schools can deliberatively use PLP processes to form an organizing structure for personalizing the whole high school experience. PLPs include many of the related strategies schools use to engage students:

- Close relationships with a caring teacher
- Planning that fits the unique talents and interests of each student
- Experience in the adult world, where learning makes a difference
- Project- and problem-based learning
- Student work as a basis for authentic assessment
- Opportunities for all students to get recognized for knowing and doing something

PLPs organize a process designed to reflect learning and growth. PLPs help students face and resolve increasingly complex questions, about themselves and the community they will soon join as adults. They help students recognize themselves as unique individuals with special talents and a history of real accomplishments.

High schools preparing to use PLPs to engage all their students in learning face a long period of experimentation—promising both failure and success. Clearly, PLP development cannot be successful in high schools where there are few choices beyond courses. PLPs work best when the school begins to organize a vast range of different learning opportunities, in school and in the community. Many high schools are currently developing PLPs to engage their students, so working models exist across the United States and the United Kingdom.

Still, there are other starting points for high school personalization. The remaining chapters of this book describe some of them, offering different ways to begin engaging students, particularly those with a history of disengagement, disenchantment, and loss of personal belief.

4

PERSONALIZED TEACHING

CONNECTING WITH STUDENTS

When the young woman—the mother of this child—stood fully revealed before the crowd, it seemed to be her first impulse to clasp the infant closely to her bosom; not so much by an impulse of motherly affection, as that she might thereby conceal a certain token, which was wrought or fashioned into her dress. . . . On the breast of her gown, in fine red cloth surrounded with an elaborate embroidery and fantastic flourishes of gold thread, appeared the letter "A.". . .

"She hath good skill with her needle, that's certain," remarked one of her female spectators.

—*Nathaniel Hawthorne, The Scarlet Letter, 1850*

I'll confess it. The first time I read *The Scarlet Letter*, I fell in love with Hester Prynne. I was a sophomore in high school, then. For the first few pages, I felt only a distant sort of pity for this woman of the past, branded for adultery. The Puritans locked Hester in their jail. They held her in a dark stone cell to make her talk. For days, they interrogated. "Who is the father?" the grey elders asked. She sat in the dark with baby Pearl on her lap, and she didn't tell them anything. She kept her silence. That's what first caught my attention.

Love is blind. As a teacher, love blinded me to the possibility that my sophomores would never want to read Hawthorne, or to find themselves in Hester Prynne.

Looking out at the class, I asked listlessly, "What does Hester's letter A stand for?" The clock stood still. Silence. Twenty minutes to go. The school day would end at 2:43. We would all be free. "Why does Hester so richly embellish the sign of her sin?" Eyes fixed to desktops.

Big Vic already had his chin on his hand; his eyelids were sagging. Big Vic, class barometer, was dropping fast. No help this time. Even Margie and Cher had stopped their chatter. No hope there. Brenda the Brain, sudden traitor to the cause of truth, had propped up her copy of *The Scarlet Letter* so it would cover up her Algebra I text, in which she was working through the odd-numbered problems. We were doomed. During that last period of the day, late in football season, 27 sophomores and their teacher were going to die of boredom down on the English wing of the high school, in Room 101.

"She stupid or something?" My head jerked up. No, the voice was not mine. It wasn't even familiar. The question had come from the back row where the angry young men sat. Bad Bernie was looking up at me, for the first time all year, it seemed. I stared, a little frightened and surprised at reprieve from this unexpected quarter. "She must be stupid, or something," he continued. "Why would she do herself up with a glossy red letter, to call herself a whore? So people would have something cheap to laugh at?"

I let the silence sit there. Eyes were beginning to open now. Heads were carefully turning, looking toward Bad Bernie at the back of the room. As miracle or looming calamity, Bernie's words had electrified the air. Ignition. Big Vic had one eye half open, and cast over his shoulder. Pressure was rising. Bernie, of all people, had broken the awful silence with a real question. I waited for the tension to build effect. The silence was excruciating. Margie was the first to break. "She's just being spiteful, throwing it back in their face, you know," Margie began, not to Bad Bernie, but to the air in which we all sweltered. "She's got her kid there and all. And, she's waving it in their face—a slut. They threw her in jail, right? They made her have the kid in jail. So she wants to make them feel wormy for a while, that's all." As usual, Margie was stirring the soup a bit wildly, but her courage added its savory tang. Suddenly, we were all breathing again.

"Why?" I asked to keep the question simmering.

"Maybe she was proud of what she did." Aha! Brenda the Brain, one defiant eyebrow arched over her algebra book, was going to cook for us. As close relative to ancient Hester, Brenda had decided to add a portion of salt for the whole tribe of furious rebels, past and present. Her algebra book closed itself with a riffle I tried not to hear. "Maybe Hester Pinn, or whatever, was giving them the needle—the whole rotten town, I mean."

The class laughed, unaware how far Brenda's humor reached. One of the Bad Boys in the Back made a needle with his middle finger and started sewing the air. I stared him down forcefully.

"Proud? Right," Bernie continued. "If she's so proud, then why didn't she finger the father?" Crude laughter erupted again from the back row. "I wouldn't give them the satisfaction. . . . And I sure wouldn't wear [an F-ing] letter." Bernie stopped, then. Eyes turned to me, then turned back to the group. Silence filled the room again. I let it sit, not wanting to suppress the boil with early answers.

A rustle of nervous movement. Then silence again. "Bernie wouldn't do it," I said quietly.

"Well, neither would I," Margie broke in. "Not that letter anyway." Guttural laughter again from the back of the room. The Bad Boys in the Back started inventing letters for Margie and Cher to wear. I walked back there to quiet things down.

"Bernie and Margie wouldn't do it," I repeated, looking back over their hunched shoulders.

"It's crazy."

"It's dumb."

"I ain't doing it."

"We could make our own letters out of colored paper," Brenda offered. "We can color them up with those magic markers he keeps in the coffee can." Only a few in the class dared to vote against her with their eyes.

"I ain't no adulterator," Little Dana chirped from her corner.

"You aren't an adulteress," I said quickly to cut off the back row.

"None of us are like Hester that way," Brenda said. "I don't think."

"None of us has babies. . ." Little Dana commented.

"Yet," grunted a voice from the back. More rumbling.

"I think we don't have the guts." Reliably abrasive, Brenda the Brain had forced the question.

"But we all have something to hide, I bet." She went on. "So let's say we make up our letter, a different one for each of us, the one we are hiding, and we wear it around the town."

"No!" a chorus of refusal. Big Vic was looking wildly around the room.

"So we wear it around the school then," Brenda compromised. "For just a day or so."

The whole class turned to me. There was a huge question in their looks. The question included, "What is literature? What is school for? Which questions are good ones? What kind of teacher are you? Why are we here? Is this aging pile of bricks in fact the temple of truth? Will school keep us insulated from life forever?" I thought over the "big question" for a long time.

"It is a choice," I said at last. "It's got to be a choice."

But a quiet boy named Darryl was already walking toward the stack of paper on the shelf. He took some scissors and markers from the coffee can. He paused, then carefully selected a sheet of blue paper. "Depressed," I heard him whisper to Dana. And then they all began to make their own letters.

—*John H. Clarke*

Source: From "The Profession of Teaching" by J. Clarke, 1992. In T. Fulwiler & A. W. Biddle (Eds.), *A community of voices: Reading and writing in the disciplines* (pp. 843–846). Copyright 1992 by Macmillan Publishing Co. Adapted with permission from Pearson Education, Inc.

◆ ◆

Withdrawing Belief

Student disengagement from classroom work is easy to spot. Passive and alienated students tend to seat themselves to prevent contact with the teacher, often along the back wall or windows. They show up without their homework, making new material impossible for them to understand. They may arrive late to class. As the class gains momentum, they slowly drop out, slumping in their seats, hiding a potboiler behind their text, allowing their eyes to droop—or possibly planting their heads soundlessly on their desks. Rebellious students become increasingly fractious as the class goes on. As teachers well know, there is probably no numerical limit to the antics they may perform, some of which may be damaging or threatening to others. One school's list of 900 infractions in one year suggested that virtually all disciplinary referrals could be viewed as rebellion against adult authority or attempts to assert an independent identity to peers and adults (Clarke, 2003b). Without a personal context to use in connecting new facts and ideas to their own evolving sense of self, many high school students ignore subject area knowledge that seems to be irrelevant. They call it boring.

In a high school where personal identity is associated with punishment, disappearing can become a high art. A dropout from Oakland's Skyline High School described the skills of evasion he developed early in his abbreviated high school career:

> I learned some English and a little math, but the thing I learned best was how to disappear. No, not in a cool way like a ninja. At Skyline, I learned how to make myself invisible from the system. I learned how to cut class. I learned how to lie about my identity, so as not to get calls home. On the off chance the school found my info, I learned how to block the school's number from my house phone. I learned not to shave—the older you look, the less likely you are to be hassled about not being in school. I learned how to not care about anything, even about getting in trouble. (Datesman, 2006)

This student later reenrolled at Metwest High School in Oakland, a personalized high school, where he completed writing and TV internships, but he still had to turn to the General Educational Development test, or GED, to receive a diploma.

Obviously, boredom decreases student engagement, but that statement paints a deceptively simple picture. The lives of students are complex, overfilled, perhaps with competing priorities. A three-year study of 20,000 students from diverse backgrounds found several indicators showing that students often devalue their high school experience:

- Nearly 20 percent of all students surveyed said they do not try as hard as they could in school because they are worried about what their friends might think.
- Fewer than 1 in 5 students said their friends think it's important to get good grades.
- More than half the students said they could bring home grades of C or worse without their parents getting upset.
- One-fifth of parents consistently attend school programs. More than 40 percent never do.
- Two-thirds of the students said they had cheated on a school test in the past year.
- Nine out of 10 students said they had copied someone else's homework in the past year.
- The average American high school student spends four hours a week on homework outside of school; 50 percent of the students surveyed said they do not do the homework they are assigned.
- Two-thirds of high school students have a job, and half work more than 15 hours a week. (Viadero, 1996)

The idea of moving through four to eight classrooms in a day, each requiring passive alertness, does not inspire many students to invest their effort fully. In addition, an authoritarian atmosphere can force compliance on students in ways that evoke active or passive resistance.

Personalized teaching aims to accentuate student identity and change the pattern of interaction between school professionals and students. Too often, adults within a school find themselves telling students what to do, telling them what not to do, telling them what they should know and when to know it. Successful students learn how to benefit from adult directives. Less-successful students often learn how to avoid contact with adults altogether, showing nothing in class that would draw attention.

Personalizing teaching happens when adult authority in student-teacher relationships is largely replaced by adult support for student inquiry, adult encouragement for student initiative, and adult guidance through the intellectual processes that make knowledge useful. Lecturing to students arranged in rows is not particularly conducive to the development of critical thinking and independent learning.

For many high schools engaged in developing personalized learning, project-based learning in its many forms provides a structure for learning that is both student-centered and engaging. In project-based learning, students face a challenging task, and teachers do what is necessary to help them succeed. Content knowledge fuels the processes of creativity, problem solving, or critical thinking. Project-based learning can put students and teachers on the same team, working together to find solutions to important problems and reducing the antagonism that results from intergenerational power struggles. An online guide to designing project-based learning units can be found at: http://pbl-online.org/.

Project-based learning has been widely known for many years, but it is not particularly common in high school teaching. Consequently, many students may be disengaged from their high school experience simply because they cannot see how academic information can be used to solve the problems they regard as important or to create expressions of their own perspectives. If content does not connect to life, many students do not pay attention, particularly those whose personal dreams do not include college aspiration. In a recent study, Daniels and Arapostathis (2005) showed that engaged students typically discuss school-related subjects with their friends—but disengaged students do not. Students were asked how classroom activities provoke collaboration and discussion, and the results from the study were not encouraging:

- Only 20 percent of those surveyed frequently worked with other students on projects or assignments outside class.
- Only 39 percent of the respondents frequently discussed ideas from their classes with family members or friends (45 percent of females compared with 32 percent of males).

- Males (22 percent) were more likely than females (13 percent) to say that they *never* engaged in such discussions with family or friends.

By connecting academic knowledge to individual talents, interests, and aspirations, personalized learning promotes engagement. Typically, disengaged students see little chance that the high school experience will help them achieve their own hopes and dreams. Personalized teaching aims to engage each student in learning by tapping and augmenting their interests, talents, and aspirations so they acquire information that increases their competence. Engagement can occur for most students through project-based learning.

Personalized Projects

Personalized teaching is based on the idea that each student is unique. Engaging every student depends on creating opportunities for each one to express and develop distinctiveness, using knowledge from the subject areas to increase his or her personal sense of competence within a class, an academy, a school, or a whole community. We developed a general conception of personalized learning to explain how personalized teaching responds to the needs of high school students, even if each is unique. In the classroom, the following conditions can promote this type of learning (Clarke, Frazer, DiMartino, Fisher, & Smith, 2003):

- *Opportunities to develop and express a personal voice and earn recognition.* Students need a chance to express their ideas as they gradually form. They need to gather information to support their views and then compare their ideas with others in their class or subject area. Engaging in dialogue can gradually reveal connections among different perspectives and facilitate new solutions to difficult problems. When each student has the opportunity to practice a personal voice, each has a chance to earn recognition from friends, family teachers, and community members.
- *Chances to belong to a working group and earn acceptance.* High school students need positive connections to others in the classroom so they can overcome status divisions based on racial groups or cliques. They respond when their contributions are valued by people who are

different from them. They want to see themselves as part of a successful effort. Successful group interactions can foster acceptance beyond small protective cliques.

- *Opportunities to choose and earn trust.* Moving from childhood toward adult status, high school students need practice selecting good options. They need to see that each choice moves them on a path toward their own future. They also need to see that their choices in group work will help meet a challenge only if others in their group make good choices. By making choices that contribute to successful group work, they can earn trust from their peers.

- *Freedom to succeed or fail and chances to earn respect.* High school students will learn from both the joy and the pain of personal freedom. They need to look at a situation, assess the risks and possible rewards— and plan a pathway toward success. They need experience assessing the effects of their freedom and understanding the sources of failure. When they have practiced using freedom responsibly—even if total success is not the result—they earn the respect of others.

- *Opportunities to imagine how their work connects to adult roles so they build a sense of purpose.* When classroom challenges reflect real-world problems, students can see the relevance. They need practice breaking down complex situations using facts and procedures. When they recognize that the human problems that really matter do not have simple solutions, their problem-solving teamwork promotes a personal sense of purpose.

- *Chances to recognize success as they pursue their purposes and thereby gain personal competence.* Students need to experience the joy of completing a difficult task—without the fear of unfavorable comparisons with peers. They need to understand how standards and expectations explain and illuminate their success, so they can refine their approach and increase their sense of personal competence.

Clearly, these ideas about what high school students need are not new, nor are the rewards that students experience for meeting their own needs. Teaching that prepares students to meet these needs must draw from the wide array of techniques that have enriched education over the past 20 years.

Facilitating Student Independence

Instructors beginning to engage in personalized teaching are not likely to be seen as famous orators filling the classroom with personality and knowledge. The goal of personalized learning is self-directed student inquiry and productivity, preparing student voices to fill a room. These teachers enjoy facilitating the work of others, gradually transferring control over learning toward the students themselves. To move each student toward independence, teachers in personalized classes know their students well. They are known in the school for caring. These teachers plan challenging projects early in the year that help them understand each student and help students understand themselves and their peers. As the year proceeds, they design classroom projects that gradually expand the unique talents, interests, and aspirations of individuals. They become excited when student inquiry produces new insights or creative ideas. Teachers who personalize learning help students find information and master intellectual skills needed to make sense of what they find. They facilitate the work of inquiry, problem solving, or creative expression, knowing that collaboration may not come easily without practice. They use high standards to recognize and celebrate the work their students produce. Figure 4.1 represents seven basic phases in personalized teaching, from clarifying a purpose and finding information to presenting findings and assessing effectiveness.

Personalized learning can be viewed as a combination of teaching strategies from three recent initiatives:

• *Differentiated instruction* (see http://www.teach-nology.com/tutorials/teaching/differentiate/planning/). By the time students reach the high school level, each has a distinctive learning style, cache of background knowledge, constellation of talents, and focus of interest. To know each student well, teachers can use a variety of surveys that reveal stylistic differences (e.g., Dunn & Dunn, 1993; Gardner, 1991; Kolb, 1985). They

FIGURE 4.1
Phases of Personalized Teaching

Approach	Sources	For Example
Assessing student strengths	Learning styles, multiple intelligences, writing to learn	Do I learn best by listening? Reading? Talking to people? Trying stuff out?
Setting purpose and describing desired outcome	Focusing questions, following questions	How should we reduce lead in the water system? Will technology free us or enslave us? How can we convince the Congress to reform electoral financing?
Posing real-world challenge	Authentic tasks, scaffolding tasks, background knowledge	Design a media campaign? Write a thematic book of poetry? Develop a six-year budget? Publish a newspaper for one day in 1922? Develop a business plan?
Explaining a process of strategic thinking	Problem-solving guides, proposal formats, examples of scientific method, discussion guides	Use scientific sampling to analyze E. coli populations along the river? Use a proposal format to seek funding? Write an article for publication that matches the content and style of a major periodical?
Opening multiple pathways to information	Book lists, Webquest or i-search guides, survey formats, interviews, lectures	How many ways could we find out about this topic? What does the public think? What do experts say? What is the administration's stand? What is the background of the situation?
Guiding students toward presentation in multiple media	Student books, Web sites, PowerPoint presentations, table displays, written essays	What medium has the most persuasive power? What should be included to make a strong case? What structure is most persuasive or effective?
Helping students understand assessment (rubrics)	Roundtable discussions, student-led conferences, project night	What criteria mark a good news report? What do successful arguments include? What does the rubric really mean? (see http://webquest.sdsu.edu/webquestrubric.html)

also can use free writing to illuminate student interests and journaling to keep track of progress and problems (Fulwiler, 1987). They can use diagnostic testing to understand initial skill levels. With student differences in view, teachers can start the task by using content that fits the individual. Later, the teacher can use short, skill-based or content-based lessons to help the group move through a complex process. High school students often fail to understand the processes that adults use to design something new, solve a problem, or organize an argument. Designing a graphic organizer that outlines the phases of a process can help inquiry groups coordinate their work and give teachers many opportunities to introduce skills and concepts for completing the task. Figure 4.2 shows some of these types of graphic organizers.

FIGURE 4.2

Graphic Organizers to Guide Student Projects

Process: Position paper (dialectical)
Task: Take a position recognizing two different perspectives (e.g., about wind power)
Graphic organizer:

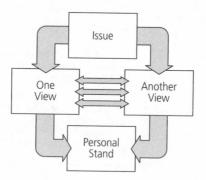

Process: Causal analysis (prediction)
Task: Research cause and effects (e.g., global warming)
Graphic organizer:

Process: Problem solving
Task: Propose a solution (e.g., for overeating)
Graphic organizer:

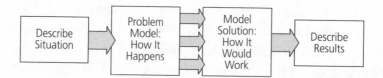

Process: Decision making
Task: Choose the best... (e.g., car)
Graphic organizer:

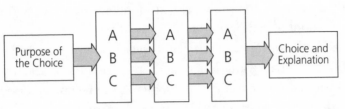

Process: Design task
Task: Make a prototype (e.g., egg container)
Graphic organizer:

Process: Proposal
Task: Apply for funding (e.g., skateboard park)
Graphic organizer:

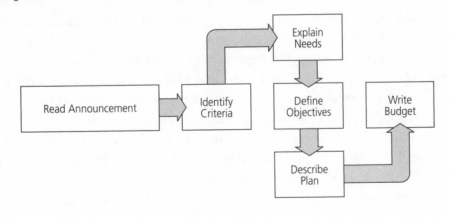

- *Backward design* (Wiggins & McTighe, 2005; see also http://www. ltag.education.tas.gov.au/Planning/models/princbackdesign.htm). In concert with project-based learning, backward design focuses first on the product that students will generate, then on the criteria that mark a high-quality product (often with applicable school standards), and finally on the steps, strategies, content, and skills that students will need to make a pathway to a final product. In personalized classroom instruction, the product is usually outlined in a handout describing the challenge and potential products that will meet the challenge, in addition to the assessment criteria for the product. If students will work in cooperative teams, the handout also describes roles.

• *Authentic instruction and assessment* (Newmann, 1993; Wiggins, 1993). As in backward design, authentic instruction usually begins with the introduction of a complex problem from recent newspapers, literature, historical records, or scientific studies that students will recognize as real. Because real problems have no single answer (or they would not be problems at all), students need to practice higher-order thinking, deep analysis, and careful planning to come up with a defensible solution. Students soon discover that good solutions depend on deep knowledge, not only of facts and concepts related to the problem, but also of the multiple explanations, contrary interpretations, and arguments that complicate the issue at hand. (Skillful teachers watch students carefully and introduce new information that either clarifies or complicates the problem further.) It seems likely that a great deal of learning through authentic instruction occurs during conversations among students, either in small groups or in whole-class discussions focusing on the problem or selected parts of the problem-solving process. With rubrics in view, final presentations can also generate rich discussions on the reliability of facts and quality of presentations. Throughout the process of authentic instruction, teachers support the work of individuals and the health of inquiry groups, reinforcing the idea that problems occurring in adult work can help students understand their roles and the way their team should work as one. Teachers can clarify expectations by providing examples representing high-quality work. Celebrating success when it occurs can encourage teams.

In all three approaches, teachers must be willing to engage students in exploring questions that have no easy answers. They must become increasingly skilled in helping students locate information from an assortment of sources and media far beyond textbooks. They must enjoy helping students organize their discoveries so they can be used to make a difference and for effective presentation to others. They should be ready to celebrate success as a process of inquiry and problem solving—on whatever scale it occurs. Because groups and individuals do not work at the same rate, a day of consultation may require working all over the room, serving different needs at different times, while students learn to organize and improve their own work.

Complex thinking has thus become central to personalized teaching. Students who face a difficult project—a design task, problem situation, creative opportunity, or current issue—cannot simply plug in a set of pre-determined answers to get a desired result. A complex project resembles challenging tasks in the adult world that require a complex approach to problems. Can students analyze the problem situation in enough detail to avoid a simplistic solution? With deep knowledge of content in view, students can begin to see that the challenges that are real do not respond to simple solutions. They require a complex response that can be assessed by looking at the structure of the argument, depth of knowledge, care in analyzing information, creativity in synthesizing ideas, and clarity and coherence in presentation. Because the patterns that adults use to organize complex tasks are not familiar to most adolescents, students need a structure to use in completing a complex task. At the same time, teachers can use graphic guides for these structures to scaffold assignments and exercises for aspects of complex thinking. Figure 4.2 includes some of the complex thinking structures commonly used to organize student projects and presentations. With a guide to thinking in view, a teacher's role in personalized instruction can shift toward coaching—helping students use information within a complex thinking pattern that they may not initially recognize.

Through this process, teachers can personalize instruction by changing the teacher–student relationship. Students gradually become the driving force; teachers gradually become facilitators or guides of learning. Mutual trust increases as students make their way toward a product. A personalized classroom may not be as quiet as teacher-directed classrooms, but engagement itself creates a different kind of order: a group of individuals pursuing different parts of a similar task. Some may be talking about strategy. Others may stare at a computer screen, seeking information. Still others may be conducting a phone interview, consulting with the teacher, or writing a letter to a local expert. Disciplinary problems do occur, but personalized teaching creates the time teachers need to manage students who do not immediately want to take on a challenging task. A personalized classroom can have the tone of a newsroom, boardroom, or factory floor, where problems occur and several people must work closely to solve them.

Personalized teaching develops over time, as teachers design challenging tasks, scaffold student work, and gain practice allowing many students to do many different things. Teachers may already be using many aspects of personalization: cooperative groups, project-based units, or standards-based assessment. Authentic teaching aims to help students use knowledge to make a difference in their own lives and the communities in which they live. "Knowledge is power," Sir Francis Bacon asserted four long centuries ago. High school students are not likely to accept that idea, or other abstractions, until they have derived some power from applying their learning to adult challenges.

Projects and Problem Situations

Most personalized learning is project-based or problem-based learning. Students face a complex task. They ask a focusing question, search widely for information, create a product that applies the information, and present their findings to the rest of the group or to the community. Students and teachers use the same standards and rubric to discuss and evaluate each presentation. If students are organized into teams—inquiry groups, problem-solving teams, research teams, or design teams—each individual can play a different role, enriching the final presentation by focusing on different aspects of the original challenge. If a team is proposing a skate park for the school parking lot, for example, one student might search for model designs on the Web, another might work out the mathematics that make a shape feasible for skateboards, another might assemble a budget, and another might do graphics for the final presentation. When the teacher knows each student well, role assignments can start in an area of strength and expand as the project grows. One way to be sure that each student is participating might be to include group assessments in the grading system. In that case, each student knows that his or her peers' grades will be positively or adversely affected by his or her performance on the assignment. When several individuals are doing different work for the same purpose, their dialogue becomes a source of new knowledge.

Although dividing approaches to project-based learning into categories is bound to be somewhat artificial, three variants currently dominate classroom teaching in high school. Each of these, described by Clarke and Agne (1997), resembles strategies that adults use to change the situation in their work, community connections, or personal lives:

• *Design tasks* challenge students to create a machine, a media project, or a useful product that serves a specific purpose. Design tasks from engineering tend to require knowledge from math and science; design tasks in media or expression call on the arts and writing.

• *Science/technology/society* (STS) projects feature student investigations of large issues that result from conflicts between the fields of mathematics, science, and social behavior. Environmental issues are prominent in STS, and war, poverty, race, and work can also serve the purpose. In STS, the teacher leads students through studies of the issue in a local context—often using the scientific method, surveys, close observation, and structured interviews—to a presentation of findings and recommendations.

• *Problem-based learning* begins with a specific situation, often from current news. Students then generate questions and conduct research in several realms so they can model and explain how the problem works. Then, students use a similar process to weed through possible solutions and finally propose a best-fit recommendation. They often present their analysis and solutions in a public setting.

To further clarify these categories, the following two descriptions illustrate how teachers have presented design tasks:

• *Designing a school building and surrounding site.* Mountlake Terrace High School math teacher Eeva Reeder issued a challenge to her geometry students to imagine they were working as members of an architectural team in the year 2050 (*Edutopia*, 2002). The team would be competing against five other companies vying to win a contract to design a state-of-the-art high school on a specific site. Each team would present its proposed design to a panel of professional architects who would award the contract. The design would need to meet the learning needs of students in the year 2050, accommodate 2,000 students, and use the natural benefits of this particular site, while preserving at least half of the existing wetlands. In response, students applied their mathematical knowledge to building scale models, drafting site plans, and making cost estimates (Armstrong, 2002).

• *Planning for urban renewal.* UrbanPlan provides a 15-hour unit for high school juniors and seniors that challenges them to develop a rehabilitation plan for a fictitious, decaying urban district called Elmwood. Teams of students compete to win the redevelopment contract. "By taking on such real-life roles as site planner, financial analyst, marketing director, and neighborhood-to-city liaison, team members learn firsthand the nitty-gritty intricacies of urban renewal. Because the goal is to make a profit in the process, there are also some hardcore lessons in financial reality" (Snider, 2006, para. 3).

The following examples show how science/technology/society projects can be presented in the classroom:

• *Studying the impact of environmental changes on frogs.* Part of the Science Technology Society by Green Design program, the Frogs, Frogs, Frogs project has engaged students in Pennsylvania in studying why local frogs are physically deformed. This long-term project provides an opportunity for teachers to present a real-world problem to their students and lead them through activities for research while they survey and study frogs. One theory is that ultraviolet rays are playing a role in increased rates of frog deformations and a decline in the population. When a class takes on the project, the teacher receives a UV ray meter so students can measure the intensity of UV rays daily. Students compile data and send reports over the Internet to contribute to the National Thousand Friends of Frogs database (North Central Region Math/Science Education Collaborative, n.d.).

• *Conducting an interdisciplinary project on the watershed.* Challenged to try project-based learning, three teachers at the Marin School of the Arts and Technology Charter High School (MSAT) agreed to work on an interdisciplinary project on the state of the local watershed. The effort took planning and teamwork among the teachers. Students did field studies and research and analysis in the classroom. Teachers noted how lessons learned in one class—writing skills or integrating maps and data—carried over into the other classes' assignments. At the end of the project, the students proudly presented their findings to an audience of parents, friends, teachers, and classmates, with a scale model of the local watershed—including trees, a rock formation, and a waterfall—as a back-drop. The principal noted that the presentations reflected on the quality of the teaching and therefore put positive pressure on teachers, which paid off for the students (Furger & Shaffner, 2004).

The next two examples present information that could be used for problem-based learning:

• *Tackling a public health problem presented in a newspaper column.* Pam Samulis, a teacher in the Chicago Public School system, worked with her students to investigate an article in a local newspaper about danger-ous lead levels in the city's drinking water. As a class, they brainstormed a long list of questions that needed answers before they could consider proposing a solution. Legally, who is responsible? Chemically, how does lead enter a water supply? Biologically, what does lead do to the human body? Sociologically, why did this happen in a poor neighborhood? When the class thought they had most of the questions, they formed teams to look for answers where ever they might be found—in the library, on a lab bench, at the mayor's office, on the streets of the affected neighborhood, and in local hospitals. Compiling a range of answers into a coherent rec-ommendation became a major class project.

• *Studying concerns highlighted in a weather journal.* Students would be asked to review the following information about weather trends: "It is the summer of 1997, and a new El Niño is beginning. Early indications are that this El Niño will rival the 1982–83 El Niño, the most intense of the century. In Australia, drought advisories have been issued. During the 1982–83 El Niño, rainfall throughout most of the wetter parts of Aus-tralia [was] in the lowest 20th percentile, with many other areas in the lowest 10th percentile. In parts of Peru, 11 feet of rain fell where 6 inches had been the norm. Throughout the world, numerous other anomalous weather events occurred" (Wheeling Jesuit University Center for Educational Technologies, n.d., para. 1) including drought in Brazil, heavy snow in Texas, floods in Europe, and a monsoon in India. As a result of some of these events, crops and fisheries failed. After students reviewed this information, they would be asked to serve as environmental consultants providing advice on forecasting the environmental conditions and economic impact of the developing El Niño. They would also suggest how the impact of the El Niño could be softened (Wheeling Jesuit University Center for Educational Technologies, n.d.).

Project-Based Classroom Teaching

Project-based learning is emerging as a way to engage all students in using information to solve problems. Rather than drilling content apart from its application, project-based learning teachers consider the content they want students to learn, then design a challenge that will entail using those skills and knowledge. New content is thus embedded in a task requiring higher-level thinking—forcing students to talk with each other about the strategies, reasoning, and content that help unravel the problem situation. The process of design and teaching can be described in four steps, as outlined by Pearlman (2006):

1. Create teams of three or more students to work on in-depth projects for three to eight weeks.
2. Introduce a complex entry question that establishes a student's need to know, and then scaffold the project with activities and new information that deepen the work.
3. Schedule due dates for plans, drafts, timely benchmarks, and the team's presentation to an outside panel of experts drawn from parents and the community.
4. Provide timely assessments or feedback on the projects for content, oral and written communication, teamwork, critical thinking, and other important skills.

Teachers need to gather resource materials for student inquiry, particularly academic content that is essential to solving the assigned problem. In problem-based learning, teachers also develop scaffolding assignments, calling for specific skills or knowledge, in the form of memos and letters from characters in the problem situation. A more detailed overview of project-based learning and teaching can be found at http://www.bie.org/pbl/pblhandbook/index.php.

Project-Based Learning at New Technology High School

New Technology High School—NTHS or New Tech High—was founded as a school of choice for students in Napa, California. Every New Tech student has a computer, but technology does not define the main purpose for learning at the school. Instead, technology simply supports project-based learning, connecting students to each other, to their school, and to the universe of knowledge beyond the school. Software called Nth Learning Systems connects students with their teachers, their own portfolios, and information beyond the school. The same software connects teachers to their students, to each other, to shared assessment instruments, communication options, and a library of tested project-based learning units. Technology vastly increases student access to information and expands the range of media in which they can present what they know and believe. The same technology helps teachers manage large groups of students, each of whom may be struggling with different aspects of a challenging task.

Technology increases the reach of student inquiry and expression, as well as other teaching strategies, but projects in all NTHS courses also focus the school's curriculum. NTHS's learning environment is project-based. Students work on projects either individually, with a partner, or in a group. New Tech teachers assign periodic projects with several different components, a written essay, tables and graphs, a Web site, PowerPoint presentation, creative narrative, or photo essay. Teachers then assign daily work, or scaffolding assignments, clarifying the skills and knowledge that students will need to complete the project successfully. At the end of each project, students present their work orally to their classmates and teachers. Teachers use a common rubric to assess written and oral aspects of the presentations. At the end of each year, students select their best work, with a personal reflection, for inclusion in their electronic portfolios (NTHS, 2006).

Through a wide variety of integrating projects, New Tech teachers design their courses to prepare students to meet the following common goals or purposes that unify the New Tech curriculum (Pearlman, 2006):

- To learn collaboration, work in teams.
- To learn critical thinking, take on complex problems.
- To learn oral communication, present.
- To learn written communication, write.
- To learn technology, use technology.
- To develop citizenship, take on civic and global issues.
- To learn about careers, do internships.
- To learn content, research, and do all of the above.

Because these simple goals represent the scope and span of the whole curriculum at NTHS, they help students and teachers evaluate projects over four full years—as students grow to understand their meaning deeply. In the Web-based personal statement part of their portfolios, NTHS students described some of their projects (excerpts are provided in Figure 4.3), suggesting the variety of ways they learn to gather and use information while meeting the eight central goals that organize the New Tech experience.

Goals, standards, and outcome measures—when listed at the beginning of a typical course guide—often prove incomprehensible or irrelevant to most high school students. New Tech students and teachers, in contrast, use common goals to assess their project presentations and select artifacts for their professional portfolios. As one NTHS senior wrote in a final personal reflection in 2006 (taken from the NTHS Web site at www.newtechhigh.org/Website2007/portfolios.html):

There are eight different skills I have picked up from my stay at New Technology High School that will most definitely help

FIGURE 4.3

Sample of Projects Described in New Tech High School Student Portfolios

Conditions for Life: In the project "Finding ET" we were commissioned by SETI to investigate the possibility of life on other planets and certain moons of our solar system. We presented our findings in an elaborate PowerPoint about the moon Ganymede.

Business Plan: In this assignment a group and I created a business. We decided to create a real estate business. I think the most important part of the project was to work well together.

Website Design: The above Flash Website is the final project of a group project I was involved in in my political studies class. My group and I had to create a Website about how science and technology were involved in diplomacy. We focused on space travel and cloning, and how those two groups of science have affected us here in the United States, and more importantly how they have affected our interaction with other nations.

Citizenship and Ethics: This was another community service project/activity that I participated in. For this we had to go over grant and scholarship proposals, and we had to decide who to give out money to. There were all types of different people that were requesting money, and we had to distribute it to the best of our ability. I worked with a group of people on this activity and out of the $80,000 requested, we had to distribute $17,000. We met several times to discuss what we thought, and then we assigned how much each group/person received.

Math/Geology: In the "Lake Barryessa" project we acted as tour-guides for a hike around Lake Barryessa. We were assigned to write out clear directions that would be useful to hikers around Lake Barryessa, along with complete math work.

Math/Programming: In Algebra 2, we had to do a project called Robot explorer. Within that project, we had to learn how to make a "turtle" move around, make graphs and graph lines and such on that line. The nice thing about learning this is that I now understand the formulas better and can also program them into my calculator.

Collaborations: An example of my collaboration skills is an economic policy speech. In this assignment we, as a group, wrote a speech of our policy to fix the oil crisis. This shows collaboration between group members because we had to fuse ideas, come to compromises and work together.

Source: Used by permission of Carolyn Ferris, Assistant Principal, New Technology High School.

> me with my future goal. . . . I've learned to collaborate, express myself through my voice, my words, and my technological skills, prepare myself for the working world, and think on the spot (examples of these things can be found in my portfolio). Tech has honed my ability to speak in front of a large audience and present my certain findings on a subject.

Learning achieved through projects and consistent assessment extends far beyond high school, and NTHS students recognize how their learning connects to life.

Fight for Your Rights

Rebecca Pollack teaches American Studies at New Technology High School. Consequently, the projects that she assigns integrate history and the social sciences with literature and written expression. To introduce her first project, she distributes what she calls an entry document, which outlines the historical context of a problem situation. As she explained in an e-mail, "The entry document is always the first thing that we present to the students to 'throw' them into the context of the project, if you will. Every project will start with the entry document, but will generally be followed by more detailed project guidelines, which could be discussed the same day, or maybe several days or a week later, depending on the project" (R. Pollack, personal communication, November 2, 2006). What follows is an example of an "entry document" for a project:

> The Declaration of Independence, issued on July 4, 1776, stated "We hold these truths to be self-evident: That all men are created equal. . . ." Yet the new nation declaring its independence permitted the continuation of the practice of slavery for people of African heritage—a practice that continued until the Civil War in the 1860s. At the conclusion of the Civil War, much remained to be done to ensure the rights and privileges of citizenship to all Americans. As America became a more diverse nation, welcoming immigrants from around the globe, problems of racial discrimination endured for many minority group members. Women and persons with disabilities also fought for and obtained laws that provided for fairness and equality.
>
> —Source: Dept. of Justice—Civil Rights Division

At this point, the entry document has served mainly to define the content and context of the project. The challenge itself remains.

After this background statement, Ms. Pollack's students learn that they will form teams to write a book for younger students, explaining the importance of their civil rights. The entry document then reveals the task:

In grades 5–8, students are first introduced to the complicated history of the United States. However, during these formative years, exposure to civil rights, women's rights, workers' rights, and other struggles for human rights has been minimal. Scholastic, the global children's publishing and media company, believes that there is an untapped market for books that will educate, as well as intrigue, this age group regarding these weighty issues. The publishing company has given you the task of creating a book about a human rights issue in the history of the United States. Your group may choose the focus of your book (e.g., African American civil rights, women's rights, Native American rights, Chicano rights, labor rights), but the topic must be cleared with Scholastic in advance.

The entry document introduces "Scholastic" as the potential publisher, creating a real-world context for professional writing, and creates many opportunities for Ms. Pollack to offer feedback or guidance to teams and individuals. She hands out the project guidelines shown in Figure 4.4 to give students a clear target and helps them divide roles within their teams. Her students now have a specific audience, a clear purpose, specific guidelines for content and process—and limitless possibilities for discovery, dialogue, and project design.

At the first class, students make out a topic request form that will help determine who will work together in groups or teams. They also look over a four-week schedule that describes the team time available during class, the movies, readings, background presentations, and quizzes that define the substance of the unit—and the deadlines that constitute scaffolding for project essays and presentations. All the groups have a common theme and common readings—on individual rights—but each has a distinctive specialty that will weave a rich tapestry as the teams present their work to others who have taken a different tack. As presentation day approaches, students can begin reviewing common goals and specific expectations for the project. The Appendix displays a selection of content and skills standards from the American Studies assessment rubric that students use to guide their project development and that Ms. Pollack

FIGURE 4.4
Project Guidelines for Fight for Your Rights

Your team is responsible for creating a human rights book geared towards 5th–8th graders. Now that you have your teams and your general topics, it will be your task to determine the scope of your book. Will you focus on a particular era of the movement? Will you divide the movement into different periods or topics and have group members (or teams) be responsible for different aspects? Your group will also need to tentatively determine which elements you will be incorporating into your book **in addition to** the required elements below. These decisions must be reflected on your group contract and/or task list.

For educational and marketing purposes, Scholastic is requiring that you include the following elements:

1. **A Table of Contents:** This should be a clear, well-organized opening to your book. Be sure to include **page numbers** of each section/piece, as well as a title, brief description and student author. Your book can be organized in any way you choose; for example, you can group literary pieces together into one section, or you can scatter them throughout the book to fit thematically within certain sections. Be as creative as you want, but make sure that it is organized in a user-friendly way.

2. **An original overview/background of the movement:** This may be split into more than one section, if appropriate due to time periods or thematic concerns. The total length should be at least 1500 words.

3. **An <u>original</u> chronological overview of important events/dates in relation to the movement (with detailed explanations and visual aids—photographs, artwork, posters, etc.):** This should include any significant events that occurred in the history of your topic or movement. Each "event" should include a detailed paragraph that explains the event and its significance. There should also be visual aids included in the timeline. *Note: the overview should not simply be taken or "adapted" from an Internet source. Your group must determine which events are the most significant to your movement, and then come up with a creative format to present them in your book.*

4. **Original, creative biographies on individuals who played an important role in the movement** *(minimum requirement: one biography per group member):* Each group member must complete a biography (on different individuals). These can be political figures, activists, workers, or any other individuals who contributed to the rights movement that your team has chosen. The biographies should incorporate information from a variety of sources, but they should also be creative and engaging to the reader. It is critical that the biographies are not adapted from an Internet biography source, as this would be considered plagiarism and the publisher would have to reject the entire book.

5. **Excerpts from significant works of literature that have a correlation to the rights movement with student analysis** *(minimum requirement: one piece of literature with analysis per group member):* Each group member will be responsible for choosing one piece of literature (or excerpt) to include in the group's book, along with an analysis of that piece of literature. These can be poems, short stories, excerpts from novels, speeches, or any other kind of literature that played a significant role in the rights movement that your group has chosen. Each work should include an original, insightful analysis that should be approximately 750 words. The analysis should discuss literary elements/devices in the work (themes, diction, style, imagery, figures of speech, sound, etc.), but it should also incorporate information about the author of the work, as well as why the work is significant to the movement.

6. **Minimum of <u>two</u> original works of poetry that relate to the rights movement** *(with explanations):* The group will need to write at least two original poems that somehow reflect or represent some aspect of the rights movement that that group is focusing on. These can be in any poetic format, so they do not necessarily need to rhyme (for example, free verse poems do not need to have a fixed pattern of meter or rhyme). However, each poem does need to employ at least two poetic devices (i.e., alliteration, imagery, metaphor, etc.). Each

poem should include an explanation of its purpose, its connection to the rights movement, as well as the poetic devices that have been employed.

7. **Each page of the book must contain at least one visual aid** *(with source/byline):* These can be photographs, artwork, maps, charts, cartoons, or any other kind of visual that the group deems appropriate. If the book is going to appeal to 5th–8th graders, it will need to incorporate a variety of visual elements that will help the reader understand the content of the book. The visuals can be original pieces of artwork, or they can be found visuals. However, each visual needs to have a brief byline underneath that contains the source of the visual (see example at the top of this page, or research MLA citation format for more information), or a citation on the Works Cited page at the end of the book.

8. **An accurate MLA Works Cited at the <u>end</u> of the book:** You may choose to split your Works Cited into sections *only* if your book is clearly divided into correlating sections. Regardless, the Works Cited must be at the end of the book, and not at the end of each section. Remember that you will also need to include in-text citations within your written pieces, when necessary. *If this is confusing, please see Ms. Pollack or Mr. Federico for clarification.*

9. **A creative, appropriate book cover:** This should encompass the entire scale of your topic as it is presented in the book. You may choose to create the book cover in any media that you wish, but this should be the <u>final</u> piece of the project.

Source: Used by permission of Rebecca Pollack, New Technology High School.

uses to assess the final books. If the class does have a chance to present the books to a group of younger students in grades 5 to 8, Ms. Pollack's students will gain another opportunity to explain general background information with their own specific projects—and have it all make sense.

If there is an additional curriculum at NTHS, it includes the behaviors and attitudes required of people collaborating on a team as they develop a successful product. From the perspective of one student, this extra curriculum became obvious over two to three years at the school:

> Although New Technology High School has done the best they can to create a successful student by instating the eight learning outcomes guidelines, there are various things that can't be taught in a classroom. Some of these values include being punctual, having self- motivation, staying on task, and having perseverance. These are things just as important as the eight learning outcomes that are merely glossed over in school meetings and parent-teacher conferences. Because how important is collaboration if you are so much of a flake and show up late everyday so no one wants to work with you?

In fact, the teams working on projects in Rebecca Pollack's class have the right to "fire" a team member whom they judge to be carrying an insufficient amount of weight.

Do entry documents, tasks, standards, guides, project criteria, and presentations—the gear needed for project-based learning—consume more time and emphasis than they should? Do the guidelines and framework documents clutter the intellectual landscape? One student made the following observation:

> It should be known that too many of these guidelines can also produce negative sentiments. Many feel like they are drowning in a sea of details when too many circumstances are implemented into their curriculum. Thankfully, New Tech High School is not known for chaining down its students, and while we are commanded to work harder than the average student does, we are rewarded with a pleasing amount of leniency in terms of regulations.

Paradoxically, the tight design that organizes project-based learning also supports free inquiry, allowing each individual a chance to create personal expression of high quality, supported by teachers and peers who understand what it may take to meet a challenge.

Because projects provide a meaningful context for academic learning, students come to see that learning entails a great deal more than fact acquisition or skills development. Collaborative groups bring multiple perspectives to the table, with the opportunity to exchange views, generalize skills, and work up a product to meet a deadline. As another NTHS student wrote in the personal statement for his portfolio,

> I was used to cramming information just to pass the next test, only to have it dissipate the next day as the information was no longer useful. So when I came to New Tech, my standards for learning changed dramatically. There was a bit of lecturing in my classes, but after the lectures we would be free to go do what needed to be done. In any other school, this would mean free time for fooling around. But at Tech High it meant getting

what needed to be done, done. It meant working on projects and finishing assignments. I was amazed with how I wasn't the only one working on my group project, that my entire group did it. Completing assignments means relying on others as well as yourself.

Organizing academic content around challenging projects makes sense to students, who begin to understand that most real problems are too complex to be solved by any one person using information from any one subject area. Several students using multiple sources can organize themselves to be much more effective.

In the context of project-based learning, individuals with unique talents and interests extend both their talents and their knowledge. One recent graduate included the following analysis in his final personal statement for his portfolio:

> I have become more mature and have become more aware of just how significant tenacity and determination will make me in the future. Back at other public schools, I felt that my main strength of writing, speaking, and creating new ideas was not being properly used. I have managed to grow these talents of mine at New Tech. I have grown here.

Students need to rely on structures that support the refinement of their unique talents. Teachers such as Ms. Pollack use those structures to foster independent learning among all their students.

Transitional Projects and Gateway Tasks

Learning to manage tasks on a tight schedule and plan with others to make all the pieces fit takes experience. New Tech students apply these skills daily in their project-based courses, but they also test them in a community setting, with senior internships and 11th grade service projects.

Internships completed by the NTHS seniors in 2005 include the following, according to D. D. Shuman of the New Technology Foundation, (personal communication, October 7, 2006):

- Napa Church of Christ to learn about being a gospel preacher
- Studio D Recording in Sausalito, a professional recording studio
- Napa Valley Plastic Surgery Associates
- Napa City-County Library
- Genecom, working in the quality assurance group of this Web site development company
- NapaNet, an Internet service provider
- Land Trust of Napa County, working on one of their fund-raisers and reworking the Trust's Web site
- City and County of San Francisco, Superior Court, in the Criminal Division, working with records
- Law Offices of Gravett and Frater, helping in the office and preparing exhibits for trial
- Dr. Anthony H. King, M.D., working with the obstetrician/gynecologist's patients who were willing to allow it
- City of Napa Fire Department, helping fight fires (because this student had already been participating in the City of Napa Explorers program)
- Martini House in St. Helena, working with the pastry chef

If all students have worked through many complex problems and projects within their New Tech experiences, they will not be at a great disadvantage when pursuing the eight goals in a community setting.

In high schools without a core tradition of project- or problem-based learning in the classroom, schoolwide transitional projects and exhibitions serve the same kind of purpose. Senior projects challenge students to gather information and express learning in a variety of media. Transitional challenges such as gateway projects in the 9th, 10th, and 11th grades create continuity over four years and prepare all students, not just the college bound, to complete a large independent effort in their senior year. If teachers do not scaffold student projects from 9th to 12th grades, then senior projects do favor college-bound students. Students who have had little or no experience generating research papers and presentations are seriously handicapped when teachers suddenly impose detailed guidelines and rubrics on senior projects, especially if the standards and criteria for those projects describe skills that the students have never practiced.

Scaffolding for problem- or project-based learning helps students understand how to gather and work with information from the subject areas to solve problems. For example, the questions in Figure 4.5 guide students at the Illinois Mathematics and Science Academy (IMSA) through two similar phases in problem solving (Clarke & Agne, 1997). The first spiral helps students understand deeply the problems they are facing. The second spiral prepares them to analyze the solutions they are proposing. Teachers can use the questions to help students visualize the problem-solving process and the strategies involved, whether the problem involves lead in drinking water, a toxic waste spill, the imminent extinction of an animal species, or the development of a big box store in a residential neighborhood.

Senior projects such as Joe Claprood's do contribute to improved relationships between the community and its population of prospective high school graduates. Graduating seniors find themselves exploring the adult world, where knowing something can make a great deal of difference while helping them focus their college plans. At the same time, a community begins to discover a hidden resource in community development: young people who are about to leave the public school system. The number of military veterans who have been affected by Joe's senior project across the state of Rhode Island is in the thousands. Those veterans can all now see the benefits of projects designed to inform and engage the community.

The need to support independent learning for high school seniors has bred an abundance of well-designed senior project guides, including some from the Senior Project Center (www.seniorproject.net), an organization that networks senior projects across the country. As senior year approaches, students work with a faculty mentor to choose a topic, set up a research plan to produce a paper, and make a presentation, often during a designated Senior Night.

As students develop their projects, faculty advisors try to meet regularly with their seniors. Community mentors may also meet with seniors studying a career field or specialty. Parents often find themselves part

FIGURE 4.5
Two Turns in a Problem-Solving Cycle

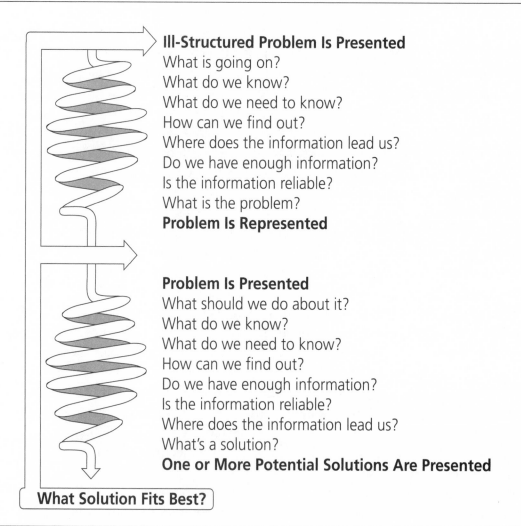

Ill-Structured Problem Is Presented
What is going on?
What do we know?
What do we need to know?
How can we find out?
Where does the information lead us?
Do we have enough information?
Is the information reliable?
What is the problem?
Problem Is Represented

Problem Is Presented
What should we do about it?
What do we know?
What do we need to know?
How can we find out?
Do we have enough information?
Is the information reliable?
Where does the information lead us?
What's a solution?
One or More Potential Solutions Are Presented

What Solution Fits Best?

of a support group. In schools requiring senior projects, follow-up summer sessions can help struggling students finish so they can graduate before work or college begins. Senior projects do add beneficial rigor to the final year of high school, mitigating the plague of senioritis that may begin as early as November. Still, as powerful as they might be in the lives of seniors, senior projects do have serious drawbacks.

Senior projects can become burdensome add-ons—to student schedules, faculty loads, and school days. If faculty time is not assigned to independent projects, some students receive better guidance than others. Potentially, senior projects can further discourage the disengaged student. When projects occur as a one-time-only event in the lives of students, the guidebooks developed to keep students on track must be long and detailed, intimidating the students most vulnerable to fear. Requiring a project with a whole class of seniors makes a detailed guide a necessity, but elaborate guidelines can prevent students from conducting research and presenting results in ways that fit their unique talents and aspirations. Senior projects that are not required, but are offered for credit, open the door to personalized ideas that can be extraordinary: building a 1937 aircraft that actually flies; designing a line of patchwork handbags that actually sells, or creating a profitable compost heap. Although senior projects do establish a crowning challenge, classroom-based projects over the longer term may prove more powerful in engaging disengaged students and personalizing the relationship between teachers and students.

If senior projects are conceived of as an aspect of personalized learning, they should be designed so that each student has a chance to explore an area of his or her own choosing. Faculty mentors and advisors should be easily accessible, possibly within an established course framework. Students should be able to gather information widely, from photographs, paintings, interviews, recordings, writings, or from their own creative work. Senior projects should allow for a variety of expressive forms: writing, the arts, engineering, or environmental design, and all the other media that adults use to enrich their lives and their communities. Assessments (explored in more detail in Chapter 6) that make use of locally developed, schoolwide expectations are a critical component of a senior project. Finally, senior projects should end with a celebration, not merely an assessment. Each student should be prepared to stand up in front of others—friends, families, teachers, and community members—to demonstrate an achievement unique to the makeup of their personalities, sensibilities, hopes, and special gifts. At that moment—apart from rubrics, indicators, criteria, and standards—all those gathered should recognize and applaud the validity of what they have witnessed.

Limitations on Personalized Teaching

Like most aspects of personalized teaching, project-based learning may not gain acceptance easily among students, teachers, or community members, and those leading the effort should be prepared for some common challenges.

Student Passivity

In conventional settings, most students learn that hanging back is the safest road through six to eight classes a day. Passivity becomes a habit that makes high school more boring and less effective than it should be. Even high-achieving students may have discovered that being quiet saves trouble, if only from jeering classmates. Project-based learning, and personalized teaching in general, puts students in charge of their learning and in front of audiences of adults and students. Project guidelines, timetables, and faculty encouragement help students learn how to learn actively. The support of an advisor is essential to success for each student.

Faculty Readiness

Many high school teachers have learned classroom management by teaching from the front of the room, where they can exert authority over the whole class. Project-based learning depends on designing and managing student behavior within the task itself, as well as the guides, criteria, and assessment processes for projects. Compared to direct instruction, project-based teaching depends more on preparation than presentation. Preparation is simply not the priority it has become in other countries. According to a 2006 study of 30 countries by the Organization for Economic Cooperation and Development, teaching time per year is highest in the United States, even as teacher working time is higher in nearly all other countries reported on. Virtually all these countries have higher graduation rates than those in the United States. Their students typically outscore U.S. students on assessments such as TIMSS and PISA in the areas of math, science, and language arts. This disparity demonstrates that our teachers could be spending more time in preparation and less time teaching—with better effect—through project design and management.

Designing the task itself, setting up a helpful schedule, developing scaffolding tasks, and creating rubrics for assessment all take time. Team teaching, team planning, and exposure to a schoolwide professional development initiative can increase the comfort teachers feel when students take an increased portion of control. Providing summer stipends for unit design activity can also produce a steady flow of new project designs. A library of tested projects can raise sights and confidence.

Schoolwide Testing

Following the No Child Left Behind requirements, high schools have been inundated with testing programs devised by local, state, or federal authorities, some of which carry severe penalties for low performance. Teachers fear leaving students to their own preparation for these tests, because only high-performing students would score well on their own, and teachers expect to be held accountable for all their students, not just the gifted. Drill-and-kill teaching is one unfortunate result of uniform content and uniform measures. Exposing teachers and others to research that shows personalized teaching does not reduce test scores or college acceptance rates (Darling-Hammond, Ancess, & Ort, 2002; Lee, Bryk, & Smith (1993); Lee & Smith, 1994; Meier, 1995; Steinberg, 2001) can reduce their fear, but teachers, parents, and community members also need time to talk through their concerns and look at studies that show little cause for alarm.

Design Time

As pleased as teachers might be with the results of a standards-based project, designing new units and revising them for better effect takes time. The experience at New Technology High School suggests that designing a project-based unit or module takes 15 to 30 hours. Many teachers already feel overwhelmed by demands on their time in the school day. Therefore, as noted before, offering stipends to teachers who are willing to design a project-based unit in the summer can begin momentum toward personalized learning (Clarke et al., 2000). High schools can hire instructors to conduct university courses on project-based design and other aspects of personalized learning, and participants can produce a new unit or project for testing in the classroom. Teaching teams can be offered a common period to use in designing personalized courses, which they can test and revise together.

Faculty Assignments, Turnover, and Multiple Sections

Particularly in large high schools, faculty assignments are driven by both tradition and student demand for courses that change each year. Therefore, faculty assignments must follow curricular traditions and the flow of student enrollment. Teachers do not want to invest a great deal of effort into improving any course if they face reassignment each year. Further, course sections that are taught quite differently within a department may cause internal friction and also challenge the concept of vertical alignment through grades 9 to 12. Creating smaller units with increased authority can be an effective response to yearly flux. Freshman programs, 11th and 12th grade teaming, smaller academies, alternative programs, schools within a school, and charter schools all can reduce size while increasing teacher initiative and opportunities for curriculum redesign (see Chapter 7).

Community Acceptance

Any community member who made it through grade 12 might claim to be an expert on high school learning and teaching. When the high school experience begins to look different than it did some years ago, community members may spring to the defense of business as usual, even if they resented every day they spent in school. Interaction between school and community—through community mentor programs, intern-ships, or presentations on project nights—can build important support for new visions at the school. Smaller learning communities also increase opportunities for parents and community members to get involved in the education of young people, through classroom or community-based projects (see Chapter 5) as well as student portfolio exhibitions and roundtables (see Chapter 3). The closer parents and community members get to every aspect of personalized learning, the more supportive they become and the less likely they are to resist the progress that high schools are making toward engaging each student.

5

COMMUNITY-BASED LEARNING

AN EXPANDING CIRCLE OF SUPPORT

Two young women took their places by silver shovels leaning against the hurricane fence, while a small crowd entered the gates of the construction site behind the high school. Dump trucks rumbled through the gate empty, then backed out full. A crane lifted bundles of rebar from flatbed truck to the muddy ground. Drizzle fell on the small gathering, dripping from hard hats and dimpling the puddles. Four parents had braved the rain. Three state legislators had come to represent the government's role in the project. The high school principal smiled broadly and welcomed each guest to the muddy site. The district superintendent stood back, smiling with pride as the ceremony began. With their earth science teacher behind them, the two young women stamped their shovels into the gravel. Cameras clicked. The group clapped. Construction of a wood chip generator and heating system for Mount Abraham Union High School had begun at last.

More than a year had passed since Jessie Ruth Corkins and Christi Kroll had begun to develop their proposal for a wood chip heating system. All members of the 9th grade earth science class had been required to develop a project and present an exhibition at the end of the first year. Tom Tailer, their Earth Science teacher, had offered $100 to any student team in the class who got a proposal to the school board for some significant change in energy use—before the semester came to a close. Jessie and Christi went for the $100. As their project began, neither Christi nor

Jessie knew much about heating systems, and neither felt driven to take on a truly steep challenge. (In fact, Christi had set her eyes earlier on a study of potato chips, rather than wood chips.) As 9th graders, neither had experience with feasibility studies, cost-benefit analyses, proposal writing, augers, two-chamber combustion, British thermal units, design specifications—or presentations to adults in positions of power. By the time of groundbreaking at the end of 10th grade, however, they had acquired a great deal of technical knowledge about energy generation and vastly increased confidence in themselves in the adult world.

The adult world, however, was not initially ready to accept the approach of two 15-year-old students from the 9th grade. When Jessie's mother and father first heard about the project, they voiced their concerns: "Jessie, you don't know what this entails." Truly, they didn't, Jessie confessed later. Even picking up the telephone to call an agency or business required mutual encouragement. "We scripted everything," Jessie recalled. Early calls to local energy companies were not returned, or were lightly dismissed: "We're awfully busy right now." "Oh, that's so sweet." "We have real work to do." Remembering that phase, Christi said, "We didn't have the terminology, so we didn't know what to ask. They didn't think we were customers." By the time the team was ready to send project specifications out for bid, however, they could attract the focused attention of local energy consultants as well as engineering and construction companies. At last count, the school board had received two qualified bids.

As the project gained clarity, Christi and Jessie discovered that they were working with an expanding circle of support, with Tom Tailer and themselves at the center. Josie Jordan, an English teacher, helped them set up PowerPoint presentations for several venues. Their parents attended each of their presentations, one of which was broadcast on local TV. Several presentations to the school board spread awareness around the community and pushed the young women deeper into the task of public construction, which required them to learn terms and tasks such as "life-cycle cost analysis." Local energy consultants helped them weigh their options and use project development software. Susan Jeffreys, the school district's financial manager, led them through the intricacies of budgeting. Jonathan Sturgis at the Biomass Energy Resource Center helped them work through energy conversion formulae. After four presentations, the school board assigned a nine-member committee—including the newly recognized Wood Chip Team—to develop the feasibility study, with $60,000 to cover costs. When Christi and Jessie were second-semester 10th graders, the school board unanimously voted to complete the project. Construction could begin.

Tom Tailer, former engineer and steady guide throughout the project, pointed out early that Jessie and Christi would have to do a great deal of research. He also helped them break the project into manageable pieces and gradually acquire a technical vocabulary. Internet research began to show the many options available in wood heat. Then, field trips to local companies refined their estimation of costs and benefits among different models.

The school board, where the team had at least one energetic advocate, hammered out a long list of questions, which, with a basic outline of design specifications from the state of Vermont, provided a research agenda and structure for their feasibility study. The numbers they used to estimate costs for the project gradually settled in. Final estimates for the project reached $1.9 million, with 90 percent to be provided by the state. As shown in Figure 5.1, the board did not soften the edges of its call for proposals because the energy team members were 9th graders. The work was adult work.

—*John H. Clarke*

◆ ◆

Memorable Accomplishments

Were Christi and Jessie simply unusual? Perhaps so—and probably not. Though they may not have known it themselves, both proved to be remarkably persistent people. Beyond that, however, their skills and personalities make them more different than similar. Christi sees herself as linear, comfortable with formulae, facts, and obscure terminology, but

FIGURE 5.1
School Board Requirements for Energy Study Proposal

Prior to the feasibility study, the school board asked the energy team to supply the following information.

The board needs to know and expects to see in the final report and recommendations the following key items:

1. The historical and projected cost of the current oil fired heating system, including oil prices and the cost of equipment anticipated in the future, and cost of operation and maintenance.
   a. It is expected that the team will find multiple corroborating expert analyses on all future projection information, and will cite these sources.
2. The cost of purchasing and installing pellet furnaces, including any modifications to existing facilities and/or infrastructure required.
   a. Again, quotes from at least three different reputable, competitive companies are expected.
   b. Identify any offsetting grants that could be applied for.
3. The ongoing costs of operation, including
   a. Projection of cost of fuel.
   b. Storage space required for fuel (how much? where?).
   c. Frequency of ordering fuel.
   d. Facilities personnel hours for daily operation (feeding, ash removal).
   e. Facilities maintenance costs.
   f. Energy efficiency level (compared to oil).
4. Hazards to health, energy, etc. (if any).
5. Code compliance.
6. Environmental impacts.
   a. Permits required.
   b. Air pollution levels (compared to oil).
   c. Ash disposal.
7. A one-page summary comparison of wood pellets vs. oil.
8. A business case analysis showing
   a. Cost crossover point.
   b. Return on investment.
   c. Other tangible and intangible benefits.
9. A recommendation for board action.

Source: Used by permission of Evelyn Howard, Superintendent.

less comfortable with public events. Jessie is more expressive, happy to engage complex adult systems that govern what can or cannot happen in any school, but perfectly willing to let Christi organize the facts. In short, they have complementary skills, the kind of balance sought by any business or government agency. Jessie and Christi learned to empower themselves because the school and its community had prepared to support personalized learning, including community-based learning, at all levels of the system. The high school itself showed the kind of flexibility needed to support this kind of project.

Tom Tailer agreed to replace his Earth Science final exam with the feasibility study. In her sophomore year, Jessie enrolled in the Futures Academy, a team-taught set of three academic courses helping students discover a pathway toward the future. Simultaneously, Christi enrolled in an independent study offered by Horizons, an academic department devoted to personalized learning. Although they no longer shared the same daily schedule during the 10th grade, both were given the freedom to move around the school, use phones, and leave for interviews and field visits. "Everyone was jealous of our freedom," they commented. The school itself made its resources available to the project. The school board and central administration adopted the project within its formal decision-making structure. On the grounds behind the school, with rain splattering in puddles of mud, the school committed itself to a future heated entirely by local wood chips.

For the two 9th grade students who spearheaded the wood chip project at Mount Abraham, the chip generator may remain the most memorable accomplishment of their high school years, but the bricks and mortar will surely not be the most important result for them. Working through the design process with their community pushed them into the complex world of adult work. "Being with adults can be intimidating," Christi commented. "They are experienced. I hadn't anticipated how nervous I would be. Now, I am more comfortable. I am worthy of respect and attention, and I am worthy of people's time. If you take on a project with confidence, you tend to come out that way."

Changes for Systemic Support

At first glance, the story of Jessie and Christi may look like the product of good fortune: two extraordinary young women who fall into a situation that leads the school to build a wood chip generator. If chance alone dealt the outcome, however, we would still have to explain how all the pieces and parts of a complex task fell into place at the same time. We would also have to explain the list of community-based projects and independent studies that have been exhibited since that time. If we look more closely at a decade of change at Mount Abraham Union High School, we can see that the whole community played a role in making their accomplishment possible. Figure 5.2 outlines changes that laid the groundwork for Christi and Jessie's project. The high school has worked toward systemic change, adjusting all levels of the organization to support community-based and personalized learning.

Continuity may be the most important factor in growing community-based programs at Mount Abraham Union High School. At each town meeting, the school board brings on new members and lets others go. On both sides of the fiscal fence, board members have been committed to educating all the students and engaging the community. Three superintendents have led the district, and each was hired to increase student engagement. Three school principals have led the school and continued to work on the same action plan. Teachers have innovated and earned recognition. Students have conducted projects in the community that extend public awareness. The habit of collaboration, rather than political turmoil, allows new programs to grow toward maturity without disruption (see Figure 5.2).

Engaging the Community in Teaching and Learning

Community-based learning uses the student's own neighborhood as a place to gather information and recommend changes. It has particular power for adolescents because they already know quite a bit about their community, they usually desire status and respect from adults in their area, and they become motivated to celebrate community achievements or to recommend improvements.

Benefits of community-based learning identified by McLaughlin and Blank (2004) include the following:

- The community provides the context for student learning.
- Content focuses on community needs, issues, and interests.
- Students serve as resources to their communities and as producers —not just consumers—of knowledge.
- Community partners collaborate in teaching and learning.

FIGURE 5.2

Adaptations at Mount Abraham Supporting Community-Based Learning

Student Support	Jessie and Christi, polar opposites, had been encouraged to form a **project team** that allowed them to accomplish what neither could accomplish separately. Initially distant acquaintances, they gradually built a trusting friendship that augmented their different strengths.
Faculty Leadership	Tom Tailer, a veteran of many experiments with personalized learning, grabbed the chance to **mentor** any 9th grade team willing to meet a community need. He was allowed to include applied learning to the structure of his Earth Science class. Project-based learning is common in the school.
Community Mentors	Because the high school had sponsored **many years of community-based projects and related exhibitions,** some consultants, energy experts, and businesspeople recognized the importance of the project and accepted their role in supporting the school. Student exhibitions of personalized learning had become routine.
Curricular Adaptation	The high school had reduced academic departments to three, then added a fourth department, called Horizons, to **organize personalized learning.** Horizons faculty members managed personal learning plans (PLPs), independent studies, internships, service learning, a wide assortment of creative projects, and electronic portfolios. They also collaborated with the Futures Academy, in which students explored careers, and with the 9th grade program, which incorporated PLPs and electronic portfolios.
Presentations and Exhibitions	Beginning as a districtwide art show and science fair, exhibitions marked the end of each semester. As students, parents, and teachers saw what students had done (a workable aircraft, a mountain cabin, a small business in handbags) all gained an enlarged **vision of what might be possible** through personalized learning.
Leadership Continuity	For 10 years, the elected school board, superintendent, school principal, and department heads created an organizational climate supporting student engagement and personalized learning. They allocated enough of the budget **to grow new programs over time** and assigned faculty to Horizons programs. Leadership was continuously positive during the period of program growth.

  • Learning at after-school and community sites is connected to the school's core standards and pulls in knowledge from diverse disciplines across the curriculum.

Situated Cognition and Adult Support

The theory of situated cognition tries to explain how experience in specific settings augments knowledge acquisition, beliefs, and complex thinking skills. Facing complex tasks in a dynamic community, students acquire skills and knowledge through the process by which learning outside school usually occurs, rather than through abstract texts or distilled lectures. The theory gave rise to the idea of cognitive apprenticeship, in which interactions between an expert practitioner and an engaged student drive and organize the student's learning (Brown, Collins, & Duguid, 1989). Through collaboration between experts and students, the language of knowledge within a dynamic context is transferred, organized authentically as a response to real challenges.

Community-based learning can promote situated cognition—or not. If students stand in rows behind a pipe welder, master chef, or 1st grade teacher, they may feel no more empowered than they would feel in a classroom. In fact, being reduced to passivity in a normally active context may feel more humiliating than sitting in a row of desks. Personalization makes the difference. If students choose their way into a challenging situation, use their own voices to make a place for themselves, take a recognized role as student or intern with an experienced adult, gradually assume increased responsibility for parts of a task, and interact with the people who fill the work or community setting, they can become engaged. Disengaged, they may learn little or nothing that is positive (Cognition and Technology Group at Vanderbilt, 1990).

Surely, the excitement of real-life challenges can engage students whose aspirations, talents, and interests are reflected in the work or service setting. To sustain the drive, community mentors and school advisors must support students as they explore different pathways toward their goals.

As learning occurs, changes in direction are inevitable. One young woman with a love for horses created a 9th grade internship at a Morgan horse farm. After three months of mucking the stable, she returned to the high school determined to explore choreography. Her advisor was happy to help.

After experience with community-based learning, most students refine their goals and move toward greater specificity. A young man in the same school began with an internship assessing the content of garbage. Within a semester, he had discovered the potential value of waste food. He did background research, wrote a proposal to the town council, and set up a composting business in the town dump, fed by barrels of garbage from the town's restaurants. His community mentor and school advisor drew back as the student gained confidence and knowledge.

Engagement in the experience alone cannot produce educational value. Value is derived from a student's thinking about the activity, with guidance from a caring adult. The phases of this learning cycle are shown in Figure 5.3. This cycle can help teacher-advisors understand the extent to which their students are deriving educational value from their experiences. Advisors then can guide students toward greater awareness and control.

Personalizing Community-Based Learning

Project-based learning in a community setting has become commonplace in U.S. high schools, but not all community-based programs are personalized. A field trip to a municipal courtroom may be fascinating, but it is not personalized unless each student has chosen it to fulfill a purpose. Mandated community service may help students see their place in the community, but it is not personalized unless each student can connect it to ongoing planning and personal interests. Work-based learning can be personalized if the student is exploring personal choices for future education and work. Community-based education becomes personalized when teachers and administrators design it as part of a larger effort to prepare students to choose, to practice using their own voice, to experiment with freedom, to seek recognition, and to improve their sense of competence. Place-based education, service learning, and work-based learning work effectively when they are developed within a personalized structure.

FIGURE 5.3
Learning Cycle

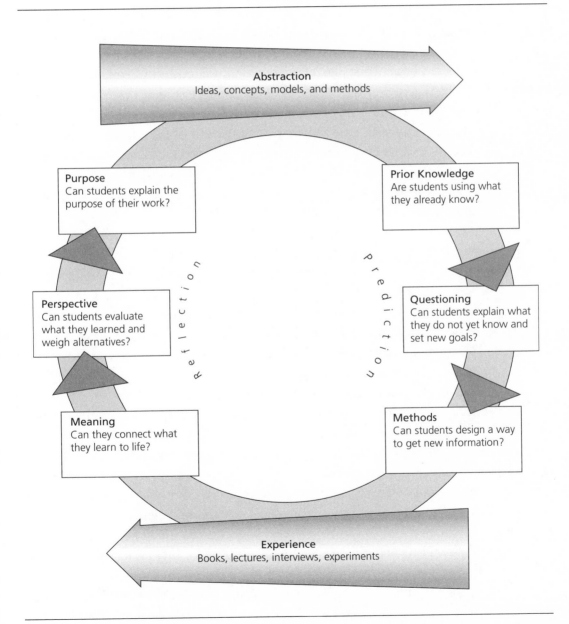

Place-Based Education

As implied by its name, place-based education uses the local community to explore more global concerns. Place-based education can be personalized if the students play a lead role in generating questions to pursue, defining the study they want to design, take responsibility for selecting a method, and organize their findings for a presentation of personal learning. Most place-based programs fall into three main categories:

Local history, folklore, and personal heritage. Students use the local historical society, libraries, interviews with representatives of an historical moment, community members with a memory of local lore, or their own families to answer questions about how the past has shaped the present. For example, they might explore how and why local buildings came into being, perspectives of veterans on the Vietnam War, cellar hole archaeology, stories of immigration, or haunted spaces.

Social research in the community. Most social research uses established methods of sociology or psychology—surveys, interviews, or observations —to investigate local customs, beliefs, and behavior. For example, students might research how the community views student behavior, what members of the community see as housing concerns, how the community has changed since 1930, or how drivers respond to seat-belt laws.

Environmental studies. Students use some variant of the scientific method to examine potential problems in the community. For example, they might study lead in the drinking water, E-coli in the river, the declining population of fish in a local lake, the composition of local garbage, or the impact of computers on life patterns.

Some aspects of place-based learning have been well developed. Science/technology/society has become an organized movement in high school and college, focusing student research on problems that emerge at the intersection of these three fields (National Science Teachers Association, 1990). Problem-based learning, identified with the Illinois Mathematics and Science Academy (2006) in Chicago, focuses student research on complex problems appearing within the community, often in the newspaper. Place-based learning is associated with local initiatives such as the Montana Heritage Project (Ball, 2003; see also www.

montanaheritageproject.org/), which publishes a quarterly magazine written by students and teachers, or the Rural School and Community Trust, which supports place-based education in rural areas (http://www. rural edu.org/site/c.beJMIZOCIrH/b.1073935/k.EBFA/Placebased_ Learning.htm).

For example, at Roundup High School in Roundup, Montana, place-based learning activities brought historical aspects of the area to life for students through the Montana Heritage Project. English teacher Tim Schaff had his students read *English Creek* by Ivan Doig and then use Sanborn maps, newspaper microfiche, photos, and interviews to research Roundup's history from 1908 to 1945 (Schaff, Thackeray, & Alger, 2003). From that historical research, students created composite characters and the letters they would have written to one another. In a multimedia presentation called Letters Home, students read the letters, using historical photos and historical costumes to bring the characters to life.

At Mendocino High School in Mendocino, California, students published a book celebrating longtime artists in their community and their artwork. Students conducted interviews with the artists, many of whom settled in the area in the 1950s and 1960s. With the help of their photography teacher, William Brazill, the students took black and white portraits of the artists using an old 8- by 10-inch view camera and combined those with excerpts from the interviews to create the book, *Mendocino Artists: An Endangered Species* (Rural School and Community Trust, 2003).

Service Learning

Service learning certainly has a venerable history in high schools and colleges. Some high schools offer service learning for credit as an independent study. Recently, many schools have chosen to require service as part of the graduation requirement. Although such a requirement may seem antithetical to personalization, it can be a strong element of a personalized school if individual students choose their own site, develop their approach, assess their work, and educate other students about the service they performed. According to the National Service Learning Clearinghouse (n.d.), service learning does the following:

- Promotes learning through active participation in service experiences.
- Provides structured time for students to reflect by thinking, discussing, and writing about their service experiences.
- Provides an opportunity for students to use skills and knowledge in real-life situations.
- Extends learning beyond the classroom and into the community.
- Fosters a sense of caring for others.

At Shorecrest High School in Shoreline, Washington, students are required to complete a minimum of 30 hours of community service leadership during their sophomore year. Each quarter, the service hours and written work count as 20 percent of the student's grade. One student, Rita Marable, received recognition for her leadership, motivation, and enthusiasm during her service as a teen naturalist at the Seattle Aquarium. After working with young visitors to the aquarium, Rita gained confidence in her knowledge and creativity and her ability to achieve her goals (Shorecrest High School, n.d.).

Work-Based Learning

Work-based learning has become familiar over the past 30 years as career exploration or school to work programs. It has several variants, such as job shadowing, internships, and full apprenticeships. It has been promoted by a variety of organizations: the Business Roundtable, the U.S. Department of Education, and Jobs for the Future in Boston. It has been a staple of career and vocational education. General guidelines for work-based learning were established with the School to Work Opportunities Act of 1994, but the practice has developed dramatically since then (Learning Point Associates, n.d.). Although most work-based learning programs are couched as partnerships between a business or industry and a school, programs tend to seesaw between two competing interests: economic benefits to the business and personal benefits to the student.

On one hand, a partnership might publicize economic benefits to the business such as increased profitability, increased customer retention, an enhanced corporate image for customers and employees, better employee retention, an improved health and safety record, improved work quality, increased productivity, or reduced error rate (Bloom & Lafleur, 1999).

On the other hand, schools such as the Met in Providence, Rhode Island, emphasize the personal needs of each student, one student at a time:

> Each Met student has a personal curriculum built around his or her personal interests. Students are guided to identify their interests and create alliances with professionals in the real world to pursue those interests. They learn by developing real world projects deeply grounded in their interests. Although interests might change, the student's personal investment in learning remains strong. (Big Picture Company, 2001, p. 6)

In other words, some school–business partnerships may aim to funnel students toward one career path—such as pipe fitting and welding—and others offer a full complement of options, including an internship of a student's own design. Optimally, community-based programs should simultaneously promote benefits to the student and benefits to the community.

Preparing for Resistance

Community-based learning in all its forms offers a multitude of advantages to the student and the community. The student has a chance to try on adult roles within a supportive setting, gaining confidence and a clarified vision of the future. Community organizations get a willing novice to introduce to the field, and possibly some useful projects. An exhibition of a successful project can be a joy to watch. Yet a field experience that fails can present a painful tragedy. Educators can promote a positive experience by understanding the following potential points of resistance and preparing adaptive strategies to promote success.

Student Readiness

Problem: Students may be uncomfortable trying to enter the adult world. Calling local organizations, making appointments, appearing professional, asking for help, defining a project, and proving reliable may seem overwhelming challenges. Avoiding steps toward commitment may be their first response to the challenge.

Adaptation: Important throughout a field experience, adult coaching is essential at the beginning. Letters of inquiry, resumes, phone messaging, dress, and manners—all may need attention before a student heads out. Interpreting events and responding to requests will gain importance as time goes on. Intervening in tough situations may become a necessity.

Adult Support

Problem: Teachers are often not prepared to take up the coaching role. They may be as unfamiliar with community affairs as their students are. Guidance counselors may be better prepared to coach but lack the ability to give credit for an academic experience. Teachers and counselors tend to be juggling a heavy load of responsibilities already, making intensive support for students in field situations hard to schedule.

Adaptation: Teachers acting as coaches need a chance to meet with each other to share stories and define professional development needs. They also need school administrators and teachers to legitimate their unconventional roles. Helping teachers integrate community experience in their own classes is a good step toward deeper involvement, if their workloads can be adjusted appropriately.

Teacher Readiness

Problem: Classroom teachers may be suspicious of programs that do not have predefined content. They may resist allowing credit for courses that do not fall within an academic department. More important, as the need for coaches begins to rise, they may feel increasingly ill-equipped to manage an off-campus activity amid the pressures of preparation and teaching.

Adaptation: An explicit list of standards can be assigned to community-based learning, with rubrics teachers accept as valid. Teacher engagement with exhibition nights can help redefine the idea of rigor. Teacher exchanges or summer work with local agencies and businesses may increase teacher confidence. Recognizing the contribution of coaches to student learning may reduce resistance.

Curricular Fit

Problem: In a content-based curriculum, fortified by state and federal mandates, community-based learning may be frozen out. If paper and pencil tests dominate the curriculum, particularly in core areas, teachers of electives may bear the largest burden of community-based opportunities —and they may begin to see their classes disappear as students seek elective credit off campus.

Adaptation: Making room for community-based learning entails adapting requirements. Attaching a course number and credit to community-based learning in each department may allow departments to expand their vision of subject-area knowledge. Adopting multiple measures for academic achievement can reduce absolute dependency on test scores.

Management Systems

Problem: Most high schools base their faculty assignments on yearly estimates of student load. If community-based experiences do not count in the definition of load, such programs cannot gain enough teachers to run. The typical high school day includes four to eight periods, with sections scattered across the day to accommodate student choice. Academic courses trump community experience, which often needs several periods at the beginning or end of the day. *In loco parentis* traditions can prevent students from leaving campus. The teachers association or union may not support these new responsibilities for teachers.

Adaptation: Because community-based experience takes blocks of time, 4 x 4 block scheduling may help move community-based learning into blocks. However, students taking special courses—such as AP English, Spanish 4, or Precalculus—might still be shut out. Creating a special department for independent studies and community-based learning, either in guidance or elsewhere, can put that program in the running for faculty slots (also increasing competition with academic departments). Strong leadership from the principal, union, and lead teachers may be necessary to negotiate adapted roles and create new structures.

Shared Vision

Problem: The awful momentum of business as usual can overrun new attempts to improve learning for students. Most parents and community members went to conventional high schools and want schools to maintain order with a reliable and uniform schedule. Some want teachers to act as disciplinarians for the community rather than coaches for kids. Many parents, community members, and teachers want rigor defined quantitatively. Their own high school experiences tend to limit their acceptance of a new approach.

Adaptation: Publicizing the success of early adopters of community-based learning—particularly students' successes—may enlarge the community's conception of high school. The faculty needs time set aside for road trips to schools supporting community engagement and for university courses and professional meetings. Exhibition nights, newspaper articles, and school board presentations can help parents celebrate their children's work. A school portfolio on the Web also can illustrate the breadth and power of these new programs.

To a large extent, the more integrated community-based learning becomes—in student conceptions, faculty roles, school curriculum, ongoing systems, and public perspectives—the more powerful and reliable it may grow to be.

6

PERSONALIZED ASSESSMENT

HOW MANY MAURICIOS?

The need for different and authentic ways to assess learning is exemplified by the experience of Mauricio, who was adopted from Guatemala in 1986 when he was 12 years old. When Mauricio was 6, he and his 2-year-old brother were abandoned by their biological mother and forced to live on the streets of Escuintla, Guatemala. Escuintla is a third-world city with a way of life that we can hardly imagine. It is possibly the poorest city in Guatemala, which means it has a level of poverty impossible for most Americans to envision. In fact, things are so bad in Escuintla that tourist guidebooks of Guatemala caution against spending any time there, advising visitors to pass through the city.

In this hostile environment, both boys were able to survive because Mauricio had a level of genius that surpasses any I have known in my life. He used a winning personality to get the baker to provide them with day-old bread and found other means to keep them both alive. This existence continued for four years. After spending two years in an orphanage, the boys were adopted and came to the United States. Mauricio's schooling had been limited, but he seemed to thrive with the opportunity to attend school in this country. He made good classroom grades, and teachers often told us of his value to the classes he was in. One time, in junior high, his English as a second language teacher explained how she had nearly lost control of the class one day, but Mauricio took over and presented the lesson for his classmates in a way that surpassed what she could have done. Mauricio made it through high school with decent grades because of his great personality and natural intellect in dealing with people and difficult situations. He made sure to turn in his homework and to be a polite but outgoing contributor in class.

After leaving high school, Mauricio struggled in college and left to take a variety of menial jobs until he became very interested in computer technology. At that time, his interest allowed for adult learning to take place. He enrolled in a 10-month intensive computer training program and graduated at the top of his class. He now is employed by the San Diego Credit Union providing technical assistance to keep the technology in all branches operating smoothly.

In retrospect, it is very clear that Mauricio has demonstrated genius for most of his life—a genius that was unrecognized by the educators who came in contact with him. It was unrecognized because their definition of genius was entirely based on how one scores on multiple-choice exams. Despite all Mauricio's genius, his background and early challenges have affected his ability to do well on standard measures.

Even with an outstanding intellect and parents who provided a high level of support for his education, Mauricio was never able to get better than a 650 combined score for the math and verbal SAT, putting him in the lowest 5 percent of the test takers. However, there can be no doubt that had he been able to demonstrate his genius in other ways, he would have turned out work that was well above the average for all students.

I wonder how many Mauricios are in our high schools right now, where teachers and administrators cannot assist them in a way that enables them to pass the high-stakes exams required for graduation. Mauricio, and others like him, would greatly benefit from personalized assessments that are both authentic and rigorous. Fortunately for some, many schools have discovered ways to provide the Mauricios of the world with a high-quality education and a variety of assessments that allow all students to deepen their learning while taking a personalized approach to their studies. Such a strategy promotes personalized learning and the engagement necessary for adults to learn.

—*Joseph DiMartino*

Recognizing the Value in Each Student's Work

Of course, if a school were truly to personalize learning, it would require assessment to be personalized as well. This shift presents a tremendous challenge for high school practitioners. How can we personalize assessment while at the same time providing for fairness in our determination of what constitutes good student work? In this chapter, we examine how a number of different schools have taken on that challenge with positive results. As one would imagine, this transition requires a school climate with a strong professional culture—one that promotes regular faculty reflection and improvement in practice.

Unfortunately for high schools, students learn in different ways. As students grow to become adults, they begin to take on learning traits that are aligned with what we have often characterized as adult learning. A basic aspect of adult learning is that adults learn well when they see the need to learn and can connect it to their everyday life. Because assessment often drives instruction in our schools, it is critical that we develop assessments that mirror the adult learning beginning to take place.

The following description of personalized learning clearly establishes the need for moving away from conventional ideas about assessment: Personalized learning is essentially active learning, organized to answer questions students recognize as important to their lives. Because students learn to gather information to solve problems they recognize in their own experience, personalized learning is often called "authentic," mirroring the processes adults use to solve problems at work, at home, or in the community. Guided by skilled teachers, students look carefully at what they know, generate questions or set goals, gather more information, then use critical-thinking skills to propose solutions to an audience of adults and peers. In all these activities, the student is the center of attention, winning praise and eliciting advice from students, teachers, parents, and community members who attend a presentation. (Clarke, Frazer, DiMartino, Fisher, & Smith, 2003)

It seems clear from this definition that active learning organized by students to address issues important to their lives cannot be assessed through a multiple-choice exam. Because each student's passions and interests are unique, it is imperative that we find authentic ways for student work to be assessed.

Personalized assessment is largely performance assessment, designed to let a whole school community recognize the value of each student's work. Personalized assessment may include standardized tests, which offer a comparative view of performance, but its main purpose is to show how each student puts academic learning to productive use. Personalized assessment puts the student at the center of the process, but also connects him or her to the community at large. Consequently, personalized assessment does the following:

• Measures what students have accomplished, against their own hopes and the expectations of others, so they can set new goals and move ahead.

• Informs teachers and advisors about strengths and weaknesses in student work.

• Gives parents a real picture of how and what a student is doing, creating an opportunity for parents to lend a hand in project development.

• Allows school administrators to see the curriculum in action, across the grades.

• Expands public understanding of high school standards through presentations of student work and celebrations of the many ways students can put their knowledge to work.

In other words, personalized assessment has "face validity." In light of high expectations, it stands for itself in public view. Although this kind of assessment clarifies shared expectations and shows whether a school community believes a student has met those expectations, it places much less value in comparisons of one student against others.

What we have called personalized assessment is drawn from earlier presentations of authentic assessment. Fred Newmann (1993) defines authentic intellectual work as work in which students use disciplined inquiry to construct meaning and produce knowledge that provides discourse, products, and performances having value or meaning beyond success in school. In two large studies, Newmann concluded that providing criteria for assessing such work accurately and effectively resulted in improved student performance (Newmann, 1993; Newmann & Wehlage, 1995). Newmann further argued that this improvement occurred regardless of students' gender, race, ethnicity, or socioeconomic status.

Educators must construct assessments that will bring out the deeper learning that Newmann described. Personalized assessment provides critical opportunities for dramatic improvement in school climate as it promotes dramatic changes in student learning. Professional development designed to help staff create common rubrics for judging uncommon tasks or projects is extremely valuable. These conversations also provide teachers with a new and better way of offering instruction informed by assessment.

A number of high schools around the country have been successful in implementing a personalized pedagogy to ensure that students like Mauricio have the opportunity to shine and engage in authentic intellectual work. In this chapter, we provide examples of the junior reviews required at Fenway High School in Boston and the annual review of student habits at Boston Arts Academy, which is tied to artifacts of student work. We also explore in detail the personalized assessments commonly used to evaluate the senior project at Francis W. Parker Charter Essential School in Massachusetts and the senior graduation portfolio at Federal Hocking High School in Ohio. By examining the assessment strategies at these schools in different communities, we begin to see some common threads. The most notable is that all these schools put student learning at the center of their teaching and assessment process.

Performance Assessment

Senior projects and the gateway presentations that often precede them challenge students to gather information and express learning in a wide variety of media. Unless all students have practice with these types of projects from grades 9 to 12, senior projects tend to favor college-bound students. Students with little experience generating research papers and presentations will be seriously handicapped if detailed guidelines and rubrics are suddenly imposed on their senior projects. As evident from the affirmations in Figure 6.1, goals for senior projects tend to resemble those for course-embedded or project-based learning and for personalized learning as well.

FIGURE 6.1
Senior Project Affirmations

Self-esteem is not nourished by meaningless hollow praise but rooted in the challenge of independent exploration into the excitement of learning, the satisfaction of problem solving, and pleasure and success found in the completion of the difficult.

- True learning requires swimming through the waters of curiosity, risk, choice, decision, and independence.
- The price of a diploma should not be calculated by seat time.
- The last vision one has of high school should be one of active, independent learning, success, and academic accomplishment.
- Failure is an attitude, not a product.
- In order to practice decision making, students must have choices. Some of their decisions may be poor ones; let the learning begin.
- Many students are as inactive academically as the system allows them to be.
- Focusing expectations on all seniors academically sends a powerful message to the younger students.
- A chain with weak or broken links is not very strong. Educators, parents, business leaders, and students must fuse together.
- If all the teachers fish in the same pond with solitary lines, only a few will be successful. If these same teachers link the lines together, they can school the inhabitants. The net works.

Source: Used by permission of Carleen Osher, Director of the Senior Project Center at the Partnership for Dynamic Learning, Inc.

The Senior Project Vision Statement at Lodi Unified School District, shown in Figure 6.2, describes the philosophical rationale for senior presentations and notes the need for teachers to collaborate on the standards for evaluating those projects.

Senior Projects at Francis W. Parker

At the Francis W. Parker Charter Essential School in Devens, Massachusetts, each student is required to complete a senior project that results in a senior project exhibition. The senior project includes six facets: an essential question, benefit to the larger community, a multifaceted approach, a research component, collaboration, and academic rigor.

FIGURE 6.2
Senior Project Vision Statement

The impetus for the senior project grew from a program designed at South High School in Medford, Oregon, in 1985. Since its inception, the senior project has become the "crown jewel" that drives the curriculum in high schools throughout the country. Several high schools in northern California have had the senior project as part of their programs, most notably high schools in Oakland, South San Francisco, Fremont, Elk Grove, Sacramento, Auburn, Sonora, Manteca, Stockton, and Placerville. Currently, all seven Lodi Unified high schools are involved in the program, and the school board adopted the senior project as a graduation requirement beginning with the class of 2000.

The school district believes that students should be able to demonstrate their learning and be accountable for the standards that have been set. The goal is to have students become lifelong learners and problem solvers. Students should exhibit good time management skills, diligence in designing and handling a long-term project, and the ability to access and use information in this technological age. We believe that all students should be able to "read, write, think, speak, and do" in order to receive a diploma. Further, we acknowledge that it "takes a village" to teach a child; therefore, the senior project is a partnership involving the home, the school, and the community, with the student at the center of our efforts.

The standards for evaluating the senior project and the content of the senior project curriculum were developed by teachers from all seven Lodi Unified high schools. These teachers designed the district's specific criteria and evaluation forms. The requirements reflect senior project standards across the country as well as districtwide and state-mandated standards.

Source: Used by permission of Carleen Osher, Director of the Senior Project Center at the Partnership for Dynamic Learning, Inc.

The essential question is required so that the senior project, while based on a topic of the student's choosing, allows for genuine inquiry that focuses on a complex, interesting, and sustainable essential question. The benefit to the larger community ensures that students incorporate some aspect of giving back to others. The multifaceted approach demands that seniors incorporate a variety of modes of thinking while planning, implementing, and exhibiting their projects. Each senior project requires a substantial element of new learning, which must include research that is experiential and text-based. Because the ability to work with and learn from others is an important life skill, collaboration must involve individuals from outside the immediate school community. Each senior project has to demonstrate academic rigor—the topic must be big enough for the student to be able to consider multiple options but not so big that it will lead merely to superficial understanding.

The Parker senior project is truly a yearlong project. Draft proposals are due in September, and the final project proposal must be completed in early October. In the one- to two-page proposal, students explain the project overview, essential question, product, research (text and experiential), academic rigor, multifaceted approach, benefit to the larger community, collaboration, and a mentor plan. Figure 6.3 shows the feedback sheet that the school has developed so students can assess where they stand in the senior project's yearlong process.

FIGURE 6.3
Senior Project Proposal Feedback Sheet

Essential Questions	❑ Meets ❑ Approaches ❑ Just Beginning	Suggestions:
Product	❑ Meets ❑ Approaches ❑ Just Beginning	Suggestions:
Benefit to a Larger Community	❑ Meets ❑ Approaches ❑ Just Beginning	Suggestions:
Academic Rigor	❑ Meets ❑ Approaches ❑ Just Beginning	Suggestions:
Preliminary Research	❑ Meets ❑ Approaches ❑ Just Beginning	Suggestions:
Multifaceted Approach	❑ Meets ❑ Approaches ❑ Just Beginning	Suggestions:
Collaboration	❑ Meets ❑ Approaches ❑ Just Beginning	Suggestions:
Mentor Plan	❑ Meets ❑ Approaches ❑ Just Beginning	Suggestions:
Timeline	❑ Meets ❑ Approaches ❑ Just Beginning	Suggestions:

Source: Used by permission of Teriann Schrader, principal of Francis W. Parker Charter Essential School.

There are four assessed components to the senior project at Parker: the research, the process, the product, and the exhibition. However, each student has periodic conferences with his or her advisor to assess the project's progress and depth. The rubric in Figure 6.4 is used to reflect how each student is demonstrating the progress and learning that have taken place between conferences.

FIGURE 6.4
Senior Project Conference Rubric

You come to your conference prepared, with materials needed to demonstrate progress.	Need----------------------------------Strength
You direct your own conference.	Need----------------------------------Strength
Your project description reflects the current status of your project.	Need----------------------------------Strength
Your process binder is organized and contains the relevant documentation for your project thus far.	Need----------------------------------Strength
You have updated monthly documentation (logs, calendar, research evidence, etc.) that shows your recent progress and upcoming plans, including: • Who have you talked to? What have you done? • What have you read (observed, studied, meditated on, etc.)? • What progress have you made? • What have you done to document your work and learning? • What's next for your project?	Need----------------------------------Strength
You can demonstrate or discuss significant new learning about your project.	Need----------------------------------Strength

You meet the benchmarks for this conference:
    Conference #1: Preliminary list of sources
    Conference #2: Yearlong calendar, research questions, mentor letter
    Conference #3: Research check, off-campus plans, benefit progress
    Conference #4: Research check, product progress
	Need----------------------------------Strength

You accept and incorporate feedback from appropriate sources.	Need----------------------------------Strength
You use your Senior Seminar time appropriately.	Need----------------------------------Strength

Source: Used by permission of Teriann Schrader, principal of Francis W. Parker Charter Essential School.

Seniors at Parker are required to maintain binders for regular assessments at progress conferences with advisors and at the end of their projects. Students are expected to represent all of these categories in their binders: proposal, conferences and reflections, mentor agreement, all their research, timeline, internships, product drafts, and feedback as appropriate.

The four assessed components of the senior project each have a rubric used to evaluate progress and guide students as they conduct the significant work of completing their senior projects. Figure 6.5 shows the rubric for assessing student responsibilities for the overall process, specifically concerning autonomy, project management, documentation, reflection, and project requirements.

Each senior project must include a product of some sort. It must reflect logically and clearly the research, investigation, thinking, and work of the senior project. It can take virtually any form, from a paper to a performance to a painting. All will be assessed using the senior project product rubric shown in Figure 6.6. Any product that does not meet the standards will need to be revised until it does.

Research is a critical aspect of the senior project. Although each project is different, the school provides general guidelines for research expectations. Research should be based on 10 to 15 sources of at least four or five types. Three of the types should be books or academic journals and at least one should be experiential, including such activities as interviewing, shadowing, or internships. The rubric for assessing each student's project research is shown in Figure 6.7.

After having completed all other aspects of the senior project, the student is required to conduct an exhibition to describe the learning that has taken place throughout the project work. The exhibition assessment rubric is shown in Figure 6.8.

FIGURE 6.5
Process Rubric

Criteria	JB	A	M	E	Comments
Autonomy • You are self-directed throughout the course of your project. • You use your secondary mentor as a resource to inform your project. • You accept and incorporate feedback from appropriate sources.					
Project Management • You use your Senior Seminar time effectively. • You develop and follow an effective timeline for your project. • You show consistent effort and growth of understanding over time.					
Documentation • You have a reliable, systematic, labeled, and clear organizational system for your project materials. • Your logs are complete, thoughtful, and up to date.					
Reflection • You complete monthly reflection papers that thoughtfully and honestly reflect on your process, your learning, your product, and your exhibition. • You discuss changes made and obstacles encountered throughout the course of the project. • You discuss new insights gained throughout the course of the project. • You discuss the skills you used and developed. • You discuss the things you would do differently. • You adhere to conventions of writing, including organization, grammar, sentence structure, and spelling.					
Project Requirements • You generate an essential question that drives your project. • You explore your question with formal academic research. • You benefit from collaboration. • You use your findings or project to benefit a larger community. • You apply skills and knowledge from several disciplines. • Your project is academically rigorous and requires you to think in new ways.					

Note: JB = Just Beginning, A = Approaching, M = Meeting, and E = Exceeding.

Source: Used by permission of Teriann Schrader, principal of Francis W. Parker Charter Essential School.

FIGURE 6.6

Product Rubric

Criteria	JB	A	M	E	Comments
Your product demonstrates a clear focus and purpose. • You use your essential question to propel your inquiry. • Your message/intention/goal is clear. • Your product effectively addresses your essential question and reflects a synthesis of your work.					
Your research informs the larger context of your work. • You gather relevant information about your subject. • Your research is sufficiently deep and rigorous. • You clearly apply your research to your work. • You place your work in a larger intellectual context.					
You made wise, deliberate, informed decisions. • Your research informs the design/shape of your work. • You understand the conventions used in your field of study. • You understand and interpret the meanings of your findings. • You can describe your work and respond to questions about the choices you made.					
Your final product is coherent and demonstrates quality work. • Your work is complete. • Your product is rich, deep, complex, and original. • Your final product shows good craftsmanship and attention to detail.					

Note: JB = Just Beginning, A = Approaching, M = Meeting, and E = Exceeding.

Source: Used by permission of Teriann Schrader, principal of Francis W. Parker Charter Essential School.

FIGURE 6.7
Research Rubric

Criteria	JB	A	M	E	Comments
Sources • You use a variety of sources. • You use sources that are relevant to your topic and that further your knowledge base about your topic. • You assess the nature, reliability, and usefulness of your sources. • You document your sources and experiences and compile a properly formatted, annotated bibliography and record of events.					
Documentation • You have a reliable, systematic, labeled, complete, and clear organizational system for your research notes and materials. • You have a record of the major sources, people, and texts consulted during your research process. • You classify, group, and label your information.					
Research Summary • Your research summary demonstrates a solid and rigorous foundation of new learning and knowledge about your topic. • Your research summary clearly connects your findings to your essential question. • You explain how your research findings will influence your decisions about and creation of your final product. • Your research summary synthesizes and summarizes the major ideas in the fields you have researched and notes significant deviations. • Your summary is conventionally sound, following the rules of grammar, spelling, and sentence structure.					

Note: JB = Just Beginning, A = Approaching, M = Meeting, and E = Exceeding.

Source: Used by permission of Teriann Schrader, principal of Francis W. Parker Charter Essential School.

FIGURE 6.8

Exhibition Rubric

Student Name: _____   Date: _____

Juror Name: _____

Exhibition Criteria	JB	A	M	E	Comments
You exhibit your project in a clear, engaging, and appropriate form. • You successfully utilize presentation aids and other supporting materials.					
You shed unique, interesting, and relevant insight on your essential question. • You demonstrate enthusiasm and confidence about material/subject.					
You clearly explain your process.					
You clearly explain your product.					
You demonstrate expertise in your topic, supported by a solid foundation of knowledge.					
You answer questions knowledgeably and thoroughly.					
You use the conventions of delivery well in your exhibition. • You speak clearly, loudly, and at an appropriate pace. • You make effective eye contact with your audience.					
You are well-prepared and organized for your presentation. • You use your time effectively. • You understand, anticipate, and fulfill your technical needs.					

Note: JB = Just Beginning, A = Approaching, M = Meeting, and E = Exceeding.

Source: Used by permission of Teriann Schrader, principal of Francis W. Parker Charter Essential School.

Junior Reviews at Fenway High School

At Fenway High School in Boston, Massachusetts, every student must complete a junior review. The junior review is the culminating activity of—and reflection on—student accomplishments in the junior year. It focuses on both social and academic development and is presented to a critical panel composed of faculty and family members. Students practice their presentations several times in advisory period prior to the formal exhibition. The junior review includes activities in three categories:

- *Academic development*—focuses on student progress over time in core courses and electives and must include evidence of gains made.
- *Personal development*—the student discusses individual strengths and weaknesses, struggles and milestones, all tied to academic evidence to bolster the arguments presented.
- *College career choices*—the basis of the student's personal learning plan in which students set goals. Through this process, they reflect on how they're meeting those goals.

RICO Reviews at Boston Arts Academy

Boston Arts Academy in Massachusetts focuses its program on what educators there call the habits of a graduate. It has created an acronym that summarizes these habits: RICO, which stands for Refine, Invent, Connect, and Own. The process is not linear, but students are expected to show all four elements of RICO in their work. The school has embraced and incorporates these habits in all aspects of its culture. Students are expected to pass an annual RICO review tied to artifacts of work they have created and show how the work connects to RICO.

Classes at Boston Arts Academy also include student-led seminars in which students facilitate their own dialogue in classroom-based Socratic seminars. In addition, students learn how to assess their own work and regularly demonstrate their learning through classroom exhibitions.

Senior Portfolios at Federal Hocking High

Federal Hocking High School in Stewart, Ohio, has a particularly impressive senior portfolio requirement for graduation. The requirement enables the faculty to review each graduate's readiness to enter the world after high school and promotes students' reflection on their education and preparation for the responsibilities of democratic citizenship, the world of work, and a life of learning.

A rubric assists students in focusing their presentations to portfolio review panels. Students are encouraged to take whatever approach they want in presenting their work, and they are also expected to discuss the portfolio contents with their panel. Faculty members intend for the process to emphasize students' accomplishments and work rather than presentation skills.

Students at Federal Hocking can count on support from a variety of faculty members in preparing for their senior projects:

- An advisor helps throughout the year to pull together material for the portfolio. A check sheet is provided, but the student is responsible for ensuring that everything needed is in the portfolio.
- Each student chooses a faculty member to be his or her portfolio presentation coach. After the portfolio has been completed, the coach works with the student to prepare his or her presentation.
- A team of three faculty members is selected to judge each student's portfolio. This team will include the portfolio coach and two other faculty members. One of these faculty members will be the chair of the committee and will be responsible for seeing that all of the forms and evaluations are turned in.

Portfolio Requirements

Prospective graduates of Federal Hocking are encouraged to take their own approach to the portfolio and make it their own. The graduation portfolio is made up of three parts, or folios, demonstrating each graduate's readiness to go into a career, take on the role of active citizenship, and continue learning after high school.

Career readiness folio. This part of the portfolio includes items that demonstrate preparedness for life after high school:

- An up-to-date resume.
- An application (or acceptance) for college, military enlistment, or employment. The application cannot be filled out merely for the portfolio. Rather, it should be a copy of an application the student has filled out related to what he or she plans to do after high school.
- Up-to-date reference letters (a minimum of two). These letters should be written by faculty members, former employers, internship supervisors, or others.
- Career- or college-related materials. This category covers anything else students have done to prepare themselves to get into college or for a career, including internships, summer employment, and so on.
- Reflections. The student must include a two-page reflection piece on his or her readiness to take on the world after high school.

Democratic citizenship folio. This part of the portfolio provides students the opportunity to demonstrate their readiness to take on the highest office in our society, that of citizen. The folio must include the following:

- Demonstrations of active citizenship in the school or greater community. Students can demonstrate their participation in a variety of ways—playing a role in school governance, assisting with a community effort such as registering people to vote or working at the polls, being involved in a campaign, registering to vote and voting, serving on a school committee, being an officer in a club, and so on.
- Taking a stand. Citizens in our democracy have the right to take a stand on an issue and have their voices heard. However, they also have the responsibility to ensure that they are informed by facts and reasoning. Students should include evidence of taking a stand on an issue and basing that opinion on evidence rather than simply emotion.
- Community involvement. Communities benefit from citizens' volunteer activities. Students should list their community service activities, including what they did, whom they did it for, and documentation of the

experience using letters of thanks, photos, minutes from meetings, and so on.

- Other (optional). Students can include documentation of other ways they have demonstrated citizenship.
- Reflections. In a two-page essay, each student explores his or her identity as a citizen and readiness for taking on that role.

Skills for lifelong learning folio. In this part of the portfolio, students demonstrate how they are prepared for a life of learning after high school. This folio must include the following:

- Demonstration of best work or competence in writing, math, and science skills. Students are required to include a piece of work (or a photograph of something three-dimensional) that demonstrates their best effort in each of these three areas. Advisors can help students choose the examples. Students must also provide an explanation of why each piece represented their best effort.
- Demonstration of best work or competence in one or more of the following areas—arts, business or computers, agricultural sciences, second language, physical fitness, consumer sciences, or extracurricular areas. Students are encouraged to show off their best skills in areas that are important to them, including as many areas as they wish. They must include an explanation of why they chose each piece.
- An annotated bibliography of books or other works the student read over the past four years and deemed important. Each student selects a minimum of three works read inside or outside school and explains why each one mattered—what the student learned, how the work affected him or her, and what the student will remember.
- Other (optional). Students may include other evidence showing preparation for a life of learning or demonstrating academic skills. This category might include in- or out-of-school activities, courses taken at college or in the summer, or additional readings.
- Reflections. In at least two typed pages, the student sums all this up by describing his or her identity as a learner, strengths, ability to pursue a personal learning agenda, and future development needs for success after high school.

Portfolio Rubrics

Federal Hocking uses rubrics to evaluate and assess graduation portfolios, portfolio reflections, and portfolio presentations.

The review panel assesses the content of the portfolio, considering how well each folio meets the mission statement of the school. As shown in Figure 6.9, the content should illustrate that the student has developed flexible career choices, has served as an active democratic citizen, and has prepared for lifelong learning. Particular merit is given to students who provide more than the required materials in each folio.

The review panel assesses the reflections using the rubric shown in Figure 6.10, which includes several of the Federal Hocking habits of mind. These habits include relevance and proof, connection, and alternatives. The reflections assessment also includes ability to meet writing conventions. Panel members read each of the three reflections before the portfolio presentation and assess them separately. Scores for all three are added and averaged for a final reflections score.

As for the presentation, the panel uses the rubric in Figure 6.11 to assess how well the portfolio presentation demonstrates connection, proof, and relevance. Additionally, the presentation must meet standards of preparation, presentation skills, and organization. In preparation for the presentation, students should have a minimum of two productive, student-led meetings with the portfolio coach. Presentations must be a minimum of 10 minutes and a maximum of 15 minutes, followed by a question and answer period (students are stopped at 15 minutes). Students are responsible for setting up the room, arranging for an approved community member to attend and provide feedback (not a family member, but family members are invited), sending reminders to committee members, providing appropriate visual aids, preparing appropriate presentation tools (e.g., note cards), and wearing appropriate dress (either semiformal or something associated with the presentation's theme).

Performance assessment is essential to personalizing learning in a high school. Without seeing the collected work of each student, teachers cannot know how to set the next challenges or bring help to bear.

FIGURE 6.9

Content Rubric

Area/Points	4	3	2	1	0
Career Choice	The folio is complete and all items are of out-standing quality and demonstrate that the student has actively pursued career or college interests.	The folio is complete with all items and demonstrates that the student has actively pursued college or career interests.	The folio is complete with all items but items are of limited quality or disconnected.	Folio is not complete, missing one item.	Folio lacks two or more items or a reflection.
Citizenship	Folio is complete with all items and illustrates a wide range of citizenship activities, both in and outside of school.	Folio is complete with all items and illustrates a wide range of citizenship activities either inside or outside of school.	Folio is complete with all items, just meeting standards.	Folio is not complete, failing to meet standards in one area.	Folio is not complete in two or more areas or lacks a reflection.
Lifelong Learners	Folio is complete with all items. In addition, the folio provides more than what was required in two or more areas.	Folio is complete with all items and is submitted on time. One part of the folio is judged to be of particular merit, going beyond what was required in detail or content.	Folio is complete with all items. Does not go beyond standards in any area.	Folio is not complete, failing to meet standards in one area.	Folio is not complete in two or more areas or lacks a reflection.

Total Points: _____

Minimum Points Required to Pass: ____6_____

Minimum Points Required for Honors: ___10___

Source: Used by permission of George Wood, principal of Federal Hocking High School.

FIGURE 6.10

Reflections Rubric

Habit/Points	4	3	2	1	0
Relevance/ Proof	Reflection speaks directly to the portfolio area. Clearly focuses on the standard with multiple examples.	Reflection speaks to portfolio area. Provides limited examples to illustrate work.	While the reflection speaks to the area, it does not provide examples to illustrate the point.	Reflection only tangentially addresses the portfolio area, no examples provided or inappropriate examples provided.	Reflection is not related to portfolio area, no examples or inappropriate examples provided.
Connection	The reflection clearly connects the student's experience with his/her abilities in the portfolio area. Talks about how these skills will be used in life after high school, and where the student needs to continue to work.	Reflection connects student's experience with his/her abilities in portfolio area. Limited connection between skills developed and future plans.	Reflection connects student's experience with his/her abilities in portfolio area. No connection between current skills and life after high school.	Reflection demonstrates limited connection between experience and skills, but not clearly drawn. No connection between skills and life after high school.	Reflection does not draw connection between portfolio items and development of skills. No connection between skills and life after high school.
Alternatives/ Viewpoint	Reflection points out other choices the student could have made or chose not to make in pursuing the area. Discusses these with respect to future plans to develop this area.	Reflection points out other choices the student could have made or chose not to make in this area.	Reflection acknowledges alternative ways student could have developed, but did not use to develop these skills.	Reflection does not explore any alternative ways student considered in developing these skills. Does acknowledge the existence of such alternatives.	Reflection does not consider alternatives or other ways of looking at developing the portfolio skills.
Convention	No obvious, glaring errors in grammar or writing mechanics. Reflection is well written and fluid.	Well written but with several errors of grammar, mechanics, or spelling. Errors do not undermine the ability to communicate.	Several errors of grammar, spelling, and mechanics, limit ability to get message across.	Multiple errors of grammar and mechanics. Structure of reflection limited; message is still clear.	Errors of grammar, mechanics, and structure made. Reflection difficult to follow.

Total Points: _____

Minimum Points for Passing Score: ____8___

Minimum Points for Honors: _____14_____

Source: Used by permission of George Wood, principal of Federal Hocking High School.

Figure 6.11
Presentation Rubric

Habit/Points	4	3	2	1	0
Connection	Presentation clearly presents how the student has developed along the lines of the school mission statement: flexible in career choice, democratic citizen, lifelong learner. All materials used connected with presentation.	Presentation attempts but does not always succeed in connecting to the three parts of the mission statement. All materials connect with presentation.	Presentation connects clearly with two of three areas of the mission statement. All materials connect with presentation.	Presentation does not clearly connect with more than one of the mission statement areas. Not all materials connect with presentation.	Presentation does not connect with mission statement. Connection of materials unclear.
Proof/ Relevance	The portfolio and reflections are used throughout to illustrate all parts of the presentation.	The portfolio and reflections are used to illustrate most of the presentation.	The portfolio and reflections are only occasionally used to illustrate the presentation.	The portfolio and reflections are only occasionally used to illustrate the presentation and are not clearly connected to the presentation.	Presentation does not refer to the portfolio or reflections.
Presentation Skills	Student displayed appropriate speaking skills in both the prepared part of the presentation and the question/ answer period. This includes few distracting verbal fillers, limited reference to notes, appropriate dress, effective use of visual aids, and a clear speaking voice.	Student displayed appropriate speaking skills in either the prepared part of the presentation or the question/ answer period.	Student did not display appropriate speaking skills in either part of the presentation. However, this did not limit him/her from conveying information.	Speaking skills were limited and interfered with getting across the desired information.	Speaking skills were deficient in many areas and not acceptable for this level of a presentation.

Habit/Points	4	3	2	1	0
Organization	Presentation was well organized, with an introduction, body, and clear conclusion. Transitions from part to part were clear and connected. Outstanding in all parts of the presentation.	Presentation had a clear introduction, body, and conclusion, which were connected. Transitions were not smooth but adequate. Two of the three parts of the presentation were outstanding.	Presentation had a clear introduction, body, and conclusion, but there was not a clear transition between each. One of the three parts of the presentation was outstanding.	The presentation was not clearly in three parts (introduction, body, conclusion), or all three parts were not presented due to exceeding time limits, and transitions were unclear.	Presentation was not organized in the required sections and/or lacked any transitions.
Preparation	Student took care of all the necessary arrangements, including room preparation and meetings with portfolio coach. The student brought ideas and initiated meetings.	Student took care of all the necessary arrangements (as for a rating of 4) but had to be reminded by portfolio coach to get things done.	Student took care of all but one of the necessary details.	Student failed to take care of two or more of the necessary details.	Student either failed to take care of three or more of the details or was only able to take care of details if the portfolio coach directed him/her to do so.

Total Points: _____
Minimum Points to Pass: _____10_____
Minimum Points for Honors: ___18___

Scoring Tally
Content
    Points_____ (minimum of 6 for passing) (minimum of 10 for Honors)
Reflections
    Points_____ (minimum of 8 for passing) (minimum of 14 for Honors)
Presentation
    Points_____ (minimum of 10 for passing) (minimum of 18 for Honors)
Bonus Points
    Points_____ Early submittal of Portfolio, May 5 or 6 (1 pt)
    Points_____ Early submittal of Portfolio, May 4 or earlier (2 pts)
    Points_____ Community member attends presentation (1 pt)

If any part of the portfolio is turned in late, a three-point reduction in score will be taken: Deduction_____

Final Score   (Scores 0–23—Retake)
                     (Scores 24–41—Passing)
                     (Scores 42–47—Honors)
                     (Scores 48–51—Distinguished)

Source: Used by permission of George Wood, principal of Federal Hocking High School.

Parents use student exhibitions to see the talents and knowledge that the student is building and to lend a hand if they are allowed. Most important of all, students use the results of performance assessment to see the product of their own work, their intelligence, curiosity, and creativity. High school students need to see the work of their minds to understand how to use what they know. Performance assessment leaves a visible trail from the past toward the future, with rubrics that mark the need to celebrate or strengthen student learning. To take steps toward new ideas and higher challenges, students need to know where they have been. Still, performance assessment cannot meet all the needs for assessment that arise throughout the high school system.

Multiple Audiences, Multiple Means

Too often, educators, government officials, and community members struggle to identify a single assessment measure that they can use broadly to judge the work of schools and make adjustments. Recently, the No Child Left Behind Act, fortified by a system of rewards and punishments, has shoved large-scale, comparative testing in reading, writing, and mathematics into prominence. Only comparative scores on large-scale tests, proponents argue, can point to schools that are failing or succeeding, so we can empower the good and eliminate the bad. For policymakers, governing officials, and higher-level school administrators, large-scale, comparative testing may in fact help identify schools doing something right, so their work can be emulated. The problem is that large-scale, comparative testing with just a few general scales tells very little about how learning is occurring for individuals, classes, or teachers in any high school. Large-scale, comparative tests are simply not good diagnostic tools—at any level. Even when tests are standards-based, the leveling of scores that occurs blurs connections between test scores and a school curriculum. Because large-scale, comparative results do not point directly to promising avenues for improvement, low-scoring schools have no choice but to reapply the same failing strategies—harder and longer—through tutoring, remedial classes, Saturday classes, or summer classes. Failing students see such remediation as additionally punishing rather than motivating.

The problem is that no single measure can meet the many needs for information that arise in a modern high school. Different forms of assessment are designed to serve different needs, so using a test score to inform parents about individual progress tells them very little of value. The numbers and percentiles remain completely opaque to them, though painful for the students and parents with the highest stake in their results. The same scores might be quite useful in school funding, staffing, and policy development.

Performance assessment has a different purpose: to illustrate the very specific skills, knowledge, and insight that a student can apply to an authentic situation. Students and teachers take great pride in exhibitions and student-led conferences. Principals can use exhibition night to illustrate the wonderful things that young people can do with information and strategy. Unfortunately, performance assessment cannot help principals create class rankings. The data from exhibitions is not comparable, even when the same rubrics are employed. A composite of scores on a rubric will not help the school board develop budgets for a new staffing pattern. Consequently, students and government officials stand at opposite ends of a spectrum with regard to assessment, accusing each other of irresponsibility.

Figure 6.12 represents the continuum of need or purpose that makes the use of assessment information so troubling. For the individual student and his or her parents, performance assessment of authentic work gathered over a four-year period illustrates the unique constellation of talents, understanding, and interests of an important individual. Colleges and employers increasingly consider portfolios of student work and narrative assessment when making entrance and employment decisions. But they still rely on the efficiency of grade-point averages and norm-referenced test scores (SAT or ACT), which have some validity predicting college success, at least in the first year. They expect general reference letters from teachers and guidance counselors as well as lists of extracurricular activities to fill out a picture of their applicants. School administrators and school boards use average SAT or ACT scores to assess the direction of change in their school, in the same way they would use absentee rates, dropout rates, and incidents of vandalism to take the school's temperature.

Those most distant from the school—district administrators, state departments of education, and elected officials in the state—use normative data from many high schools to make policy decisions and formulate political arguments. The audiences for assessment data are many, but their needs are not at all the same.

FIGURE 6.12
Multiple Assessment Needs and Multiple Audiences

	Audience for Assessment Information	Purpose of Assessment Process	Assessment Process and Indicators
Personal Data (Validity)	**Students and parents:** What are my options and choices for the future?	**Goal setting:** To gain clarity about student interests, talents, and aspirations in relation to realistic life goals	**Performance assessment:** Exhibitions, portfolios, standards-based rubrics, grades in different subjects
	Teachers and school services: What is the evidence of academic progress?	**Fit with the curriculum:** Movement toward standards and school expectations	**Academic assessment:** Student performance and knowledge acquisition in a subject area— grades, projects, and written work, SAT scores
↕	**School administrators:** Is the school educating the kids well?	**Management process:** Evidence of effectiveness	**Comparative markers:** SAT average, number of college applications and acceptances, recognition and awards for programs, vandalism, surveys, absenteeism, graduation rates
Comparative Data (Reliability)	**District administrators and school board:** Are the schools spending responsibly?	**System and structure:** Evidence of efficiency	**Comparative trends:** Budget expansion, student population, enrollment patterns, large-scale, comparative test score patterns
	State education departments and elected officials: Are we getting what we want?	**Accountability:** Evidence of value	**Comparative value:** Large-scale, comparative tests scores; per-pupil expenditures; costs and benefits

Surely, the lines dividing levels of the system can seriously misrepresent the different uses of assessment data. Parents and senators may both be interested in per-pupil expenditures in a high school. Both could be equally interested in a student project on waste management. The figure does reveal the structure of a real problem in assessment: the need for assessment data throughout the system is so pressing that different needs compete for the most essential resource there is in high school learning—time.

Budgets may rise and fall, but time arranges itself the same way each and every day. How should we spend precious time within the school day? We could spend it helping students prepare a presentation in algebra and science, or we could review items from the latest version of a norm-referenced test that will determine whether we are identified as a failing school. We could adjust the assessment system to favor personalized assessment, featuring student work, or we could force students into two sections of algebra to push up their scores.

Personalized high schools clearly favor authentic assessment of student work. Without projects, presentations, rubrics, and portfolios, personalized learning cannot happen. Some personalized high schools keep the personalized structure intact but move failing students into special classes or tutorials to try getting the numbers up. Other personalized schools spend a week or so with advisory groups, going over the kinds of items that show up on large-scale, comparative tests. Other personalized high schools, believing that student engagement, self-direction, and personalized learning will compensate for any lack of interest in large-scale, comparative tests, simply set up the test rooms, cheer the students on, and wait for the normal curve to generate a number they will all have to live with. In either case, competition between personalized assessment and comparative testing can force everyone in school to take a side, depriving the school as a whole of its ability to engage each student.

Recognizing the wild array of differences among high school students, personalized learning accentuates the special talents, interests, and aspirations of each student. Personalized assessment illuminates student strengths, rather than focusing on weaknesses. Comparing different students on personalized measures would be feckless. Norm-referenced assessments, and many standards-based tests, focus on differences among students. Weakness within a general area is easy to spot, if not to understand. Special talents and interests do not appear at all in the results of large-scale tests. When advocates of accountability impose strict testing requirements on high schools, they devalue the most powerful motivator among adolescents and young adults: the chance to be recognized as competent and unique within a supportive school. As communities work to understand personalized assessment and large-scale testing in their schools, they will need to determine what really matters: numbers on a printout or student work in a portfolio. Then they can face the issues that arise in the battle for time.

7

Personalizing School Systems

New Hampshire and the Carnegie Unit

More than a century ago, during the first U.S. wave of standardization, the Carnegie Foundation for the Advancement of Teaching proposed a system to standardize high school credits by assigning one unit of value to a subject taught one hour a day, five days a week, for one school year. Since then, the Carnegie unit has admirably performed its singular purpose: transforming the ambiguities of education into a clear set of inputs, outputs, and calculations. Seat time yields credits; credits yield a diploma.

During the last 20 years, the Carnegie unit has come under widespread criticism. In fact, it was disowned by its family when the Carnegie Foundation's then-president, Ernest Boyer, "officially declare[d] the Carnegie unit obsolete" (Boyer, 1993). But despite its increasingly unwelcome and counterproductive place in U.S. high schools, the Carnegie unit persists because it has successfully taken control of the most intransigent elements of these schools: scheduling, grading, staffing, higher education admissions, and the four-year sequenced curriculum.

The Carnegie unit and authentic assessment are unhappy bedfellows. A seven-period school day can be neatly divided into disciplines and tidily equated with Carnegie units, but it cripples the most prevalent forms of authentic assessment. Teaching and assessing through senior projects, exhibitions, portfolios, and capstone projects require multidisciplinary, extended learning time that collides with a seven-period day or even a 4 x 4 block schedule. To integrate authentic assessment and the prevailing Carnegie unit system, administrators and teachers must perform instructional and logistical gymnastics to address difficult questions: Is a student project worth "credits"? If so, how many? What core content areas should long-term student projects count toward? How does student performance on authentic assessments fit into classroom grades—or do such assessments render letter grades obsolete? How do we create transcripts that reflect student proficiency on authentic assessments, and will colleges and universities accept them? These questions, and the time and effort required to answer them, aren't about pedagogy or even about education. They are about compliance with an anachronistic system that schools seem reluctant to retire.

Unfortunately, for the foreseeable future, the Carnegie unit is likely to persist as the structuring principle of U.S. high schools. Within these staid parameters, however, educators have found ways to use authentic instruction and assessment to create well-rounded students. These innovators use, adapt, and in some cases subvert the Carnegie unit system in an effort to transform their students into prepared graduates.

In 2005, New Hampshire became the first state to formally eliminate the Carnegie unit. The New Hampshire Board of Education has directed every school district in the state to design and implement a competency-based system that will allow students to earn credits—and diplomas—through a process ungoverned by the 120-hour Carnegie unit requirement. This new system moves authentic assessment from the trunk of the car to the driver's seat, where it will now serve as the predominant mechanism for awarding student credit both in and out of the classroom.

Within the broad scope of local control, New Hampshire's new education regulations contain a small but crucial set of established parameters. First, districts must identify core competencies and establish authentic assessments to evaluate student mastery of those competencies for every high school course. Second, districts must provide the state department of education with evidence that they've established and implemented a competency assessment system that is grounded in appropriate local and national standards. If they address these two requirements, districts will be

largely free to change or retain virtually any of the structuring and scheduling elements typical of secondary education.

Few school districts in New Hampshire are ready to tackle these
daunting challenges immediately; many are moving forward cautiously,
creating limited and carefully defined approaches to authentic teaching
and assessment. A significant number of administrators, however, have
welcomed the new policy as the long-absent lever that will force real,
lasting, schoolwide improvement. These leaders, most of whom have
been working to develop authentic assessments for years, are beginning
to implement new and varied methods for awarding students academic
credit.

—*Joseph DiMartino and Andrea Castaneda*

Reprinted in adapted form from DiMartino, J., & Castaneda, A. (2007, April). Assessing applied skills
[online article]. *Educational Leadership*, 64(7), para. 9–12 and 28–30. Available: www.ascd.org/

❖ ❖

Aiming to Improve Quality

Surely, the advocates of comprehensive high schools between 1920 and
1940 did not set out to alienate a large proportion of their students.
Instead, as part of the Progressive movement, they wanted to improve
the quality of secondary schools for all U.S. students. Early reformers
were particularly concerned that students in many rural schools had only
one teacher, limiting the depth of instruction in classes and spreading
the tasks of supervision and administration over a wide geographic area.
Larger schools promised more efficient, centralized, and professional
administration. Comprehensive high schools also created the opportunity for specialized teaching in depth, by subject area, grade, and ability level—promising to improve the quality of education. Finally, large
buildings housing thousands of students and hundreds of adults increased
the options for students at a lower cost than hundreds of schools trying to
provide the same services in one small space. Consolidating high schools
offered economies of scale in administration, instruction, and facilities

(Berry, 2007). At the same time, building high schools across the country on the same basic model would allow students to migrate from school to school without noticing major differences.

Aiming to increase efficiency and rationality and reduce costs, the industrial model also produced unintended secondary effects that contributed to high dropout rates. Centralizing and professionalizing the administration of schools led to the massive bureaucracies that manage state departments of education and large school districts today—separating schools from the communities they were meant to serve. Assigning teachers to specialty subject areas and curriculum based on scope and sequence divided the high school experience into silos—by grade levels, subject areas, and tracks—reducing the chance that teachers and students get to know one another. Facilities designed to partition a wide assortment of separate learning experiences also helped create the sprawling labyrinths of halls and rooms that now guard the anonymity of students and teachers alike, while isolating students from the outside world where they so desperately want to find a fitting place. Surely, James Conant, the former president of Harvard University, and his predecessors whose recommendations led to the Carnegie unit had worthy motives. Did the reformers of early times hope their reforms would prove permanent? They surely have proven durable, making the process of continuing reform remarkably difficult and frustrating.

The Awful Momentum of Business as Usual

Change from within a large and impersonal high school is difficult because the large system was designed with interlocking parts. Students graduate when they have accumulated prescribed Carnegie units across a variety of subject areas. Teachers are licensed to teach in just one or two of those subjects, limiting their ability to adapt. State law often prohibits teaching outside a subject area. Academic departments have formed to define a curriculum and protect it from wild variation. Each subject area is assigned one period each day to cover just one small portion of that curriculum. In the name of equity, teacher unions insist on contracts that are uniform across the curriculum, preventing double assignments that could support change. Principals must supervise teachers in each subject area, even if they have no acquaintance with the discipline, so they apply generic standards to all teachers. State departments of education call out for change, but they also impose rules, regulations, and procedures that make change impossible. In short, each piece of the high school system is inextricably connected to other pieces, similar to the Gordian knot shown in Figure 7.1. Locked into place by law and tradition, the whole enterprise has become too uniform to work well for each student and too unwieldy for any individual to change. "Trying to change one piece affects every other," said Theodore Sizer (1984, p. 211), and enormous size makes significant change virtually impossible.

FIGURE 7.1
Interlocking Systems

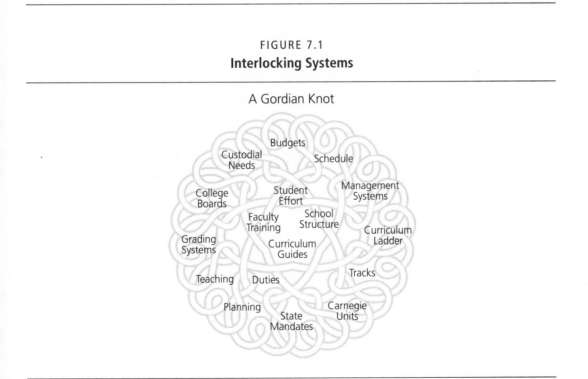

As a result, attempts at personalizing large high schools often last no longer than the innovators who organize them. Personalized learning requires a different kind of organization than a rational bureaucracy.

Large schools trying to engage each student can find themselves running two systems at once, academic departments and cross-disciplinary teaching teams, for example, or a hierarchical management system and a network of distributed leadership where all members of the community have some leadership responsibility. A changing school may need a line-item budget to get the bills paid and a program budget to support program development—twice the effort for the same work. Adding a personalized program to a conventional structure adds another expense as well as another burden to an overloaded schedule. In the daily press of activity in a large school system, schools tend to swing back to business as usual, to processes and procedures that maintain old ways but starve early efforts to personalize high school learning.

These early efforts to engage each student in a large high school can look glorious at the onset and tragic thereafter.

In one rural community, high school innovators had created a popular community-based learning program for students. Students spread across the county. With that program well established, school leaders turned to personal learning plans (PLPs) to engage all students. The faculty began to resist, arguing that they should aim to improve what they already had before adding new projects. Traditional educators won the day, and the faculty then spent the following years refining the subject-area curriculum. Personalized learning and teaching slowly disappeared from public dialogue. The faculty had been persuaded that students would benefit from community engagement, but they would not support a PLP initiative that would add to their burdens.

Another rural high school began an effort to personalize the curriculum based on authentic tasks and standards-based assessment. Over a period of two years, faculty and students developed and tested a number of interesting subject-based projects. Soon, however, dynamic leaders in the faculty and administration received job offers from other schools that were interested in personalized learning. Leadership evaporated as reform-minded educators migrated out to districts where they expected to receive a clear mandate for change and an easier path. Project-based learning withered and died.

In an urban high school, community-based learning quickly expanded between students and local business, service, and government offices. With students earning credit all over the city, it seemed natural to introduce PLPs and an advisory that would help each student explore adult roles. Expansion proceeded throughout the school, until a beloved principal retired and faculty leaders either collapsed or departed. Except for the community-based learning program and some isolated projects, personalized learning began to shrink.

In a large high school with interdependent parts, personalization requires a "yes" from each individual, but derailing a personalization initiative needs just one loud voice saying "no." The systems we have developed to organize very large institutions cannot support the kind of education that helps each student pursue a personal pathway (with PLPs), safely explore multiple options (with advisors), use information to make a difference (with project-based learning), assemble evidence of achievement (with portfolios), present new ideas to the whole community (with exhibitions), or engage the adult community in educating emerging adults (with internships or service projects).

What happened to these promising plans? Briefly, they died of starvation (Clarke et al., 2000). The systems established to support conventional teaching and learning did not adapt to support student-centered, personalized learning. Instead, they continued supporting conventional ways of teaching and learning, which rolled along relentlessly, driven by 50 years of momentum. To the consternation of many reformers, high school systems are systems: functions and activities woven together to support a narrowly defined (and tightly funded) purpose. Typically, high schools devote very little of the budget to innovation.

Particularly after the movement toward district unification, comprehensive high schools grew into very large systems indeed, designed to distribute discrete functions to academic departments and support services with exactitude. New needs among students generated new courses and new services. The system grew larger and more elaborate, but the structure did not change. Students entering a public high school often cannot comprehend the system in which they are enmeshed. Things just happen to them; they don't know why. They don't feel empowered to influence their own pathways. Some drift. Some drop out. Some persist toward college. If high school curricula are designed to prepare students for college, the relatively low college placement rate suggests that schools may have become highly efficient with sparse resources, but not very effective with all the students they aim to serve.

Preparing a Monolith for Change

Change must grow inside a community of students, parents, and teachers who are not satisfied with the current level of practice and are determined to experiment with new techniques. They need to develop a new mission and goals. If policy is to support the evolution of improved practice, it must first reduce the restrictive effects that existing policy has on knowledge development and dissemination within the teaching profession. Teachers need time to develop their art and to talk with each other about the challenges they face. They need resources that will let them learn how to test one idea against another in the living context of their own classes. Most of all, they need to recognize that responsibility for the improvement of teaching and learning lies not with policymakers in the political arena, but in the schools where they are learning to become an adaptive, self-organizing profession. The development of personalized learning and student engagement depends on a new design for high school systems.

The need for systemic change is reflected in the three high school reform efforts that are currently making a significant difference in high school learning. Sizer (1984) recognized the necessity of rebuilding the system when he developed the principles of the Coalition of Essential Schools, calling for reduced size and much greater support for individual students. The result was a large number of small schools—alternative schools, charter schools, magnet schools, and schools of choice that pull students and teachers from the large system but leave it otherwise intact. Large schools—like highly complex organisms in nature—do not adapt as readily as smaller schools, which can be more flexible. Seeing the system as a hierarchical structure in which responsibility and resources are handed down to departments and offices while information is fed up prevents us from seeing promising ways to engage all students in learning. Seeing high school as a learning community opens doors to new options.

With specialized functions packed into every nook and cranny, hierarchical or rational systems can add more functions—becoming increasingly unwieldy—but they cannot remake themselves into personalized learning communities. How can large high schools reduce the alienating effects that result from size and complexity?

Converting Large Schools to Personalized Learning Communities

We believe that you can't reform high schools. You have to rebuild them. A corollary might be, "If you rebuild your high school the same way it was built, you won't get different results." To engage all students in learning, as previous chapters have shown, we need a different kind of high school. We have called that a personalized high school, a place where students discover their own pathways to the future, where teachers act as advisors to their students, where teachers pose real problems for their students to solve by applying subject area knowledge, where students demonstrate their mastery of subjects and skills through portfolios and exhibitions—and where all members of the school community work together to help each member succeed. That kind of high school cannot be the gigantic organization of several thousand students called the comprehensive high school. Breaking down large structures into smaller schools brings students, teachers, administrators, and community members into contact within a manageable group, so they can pursue a vision they all share.

High schools may simply miniaturize their bureaucratic shape—and their bureaucratic problems—unless smaller forms are accompanied by intellectual growth. In short, to personalize learning, all members of the high school community need to change their concept of a high school. To do that, they need to begin an ongoing process of dialogue across the boundaries that divide their school. Each individual needs the time and support to adapt old ideas and adopt new ideas in concert with others who are also changing their conceptions. That change constitutes a para-digm shift, a vision of high school learning based on individual planning, close relationships between adults and students, teaching that prepares students to acquire knowledge and use it to create new ideas or solve problems, and interaction with the community in ways that help students understand adult roles.

Rebuilding U.S. high schools will require what Peter Senge has called a systems perspective (1990). To take responsibility for change, all mem-bers of the school community should develop the ability to understand the school as a system. Systems thinking is a way of thinking about, and a language for describing and understanding, the forces and interrelation-ships that shape the behavior of systems. The practice of this discipline develops awareness of complexity, interdependencies, change, and leverage.

When a school community has developed a shared vision and a sys-tems perspective, it can begin to gather leadership density that becomes possible when every member of the community leads some part of the learning process: students lead teachers and parents through portfolio assessment; advisors lead students to discover personal pathways; teach-ers lead inquiry projects; and community mentors lead students toward adult roles. With shared vision, systems thinking, and leadership density, a school can design new structures for its work. Those three components of active change become more easily achievable in a smaller school than a larger one. Breaking enormous comprehensive high schools into smaller academies, institutes, or communities can create a manageable structure where personalized learning can grow.

The five new academies at Mountlake Terrace High School in Mountlake Terrace, Washington—described in Figure 7.2—serve as an example. Designed by the community to attract distinctive students, the academies survived a tumultuous birth and now reflect different per-sonalities. Some high schools have chosen to develop career academies tracked toward different occupations. Others have chosen academic themes, such as technology, humanities, or the arts. Some have simply developed randomized communities with distinctive names.

FIGURE 7.2
Five Academies at Mountlake Terrace High School

The Discovery School
At the Discovery School we are passionate about making education meaningful, challenging, and fun—simultaneously! We are a school that honors and celebrates your strengths and interests. We are a school that emphasizes positive relationships among students, staff, parents, and community members. We are a school where you frequently design your own projects with direction from teachers, through innovative class sessions as well as through traditional courses. We are a school that values meeting regularly to grapple with meaningful questions, seek and secure academic assistance, serve our community, and develop lasting relationships.

The Innovation School

We are creative thinkers
We admire people who like to think and do things differently. Our role models include the Wright Brothers, Albert Einstein, Pablo Picasso, Maya Angelou. We cultivate creative problem-solving skills and technological savvy, so that we can make responsible and positive changes in our world.

We are writers and speakers, artists and inventors
We are scholars, craftsmen, and citizens in an ever-changing world. We express ourselves in traditional and innovative ways, including art, poetry, and design. We learn how to communicate in-depth learning through good writing, speaking, and presentation skills.

We are energetic and involved
We are involved in fun and exciting student-centered activities such as the Innovation girls' sleepover, the Garage Cafe, the Design and Destruct Team, and field trips to places such as the Museum of Flight and the USS Carl Vinson aircraft carrier.

We are diverse
We celebrate different backgrounds, interests, and learning styles. We draw on contributions from all cultures, races, and ethnicities. Our creativity is expanded by diverse points of view.

The Renaissance School
Botticelli, Shakespeare, Galileo, daVinci . . . If you ask any artist they will most certainly identify each of these individuals as a remarkable artist. Approach scientists or scholars on the matter, and they will undoubtedly point out the many academic achievements of each. The Renaissance School is devoted to providing an environment in which students can explore the interconnections between academics and performing arts. In this fashion, students will discover the importance of developing knowledge in all disciplines in order to truly excel at that which they love most.

Terrace Arts and Academics School
We are a college prep school founded on the belief that academic challenge and the study of the arts prepare students to live rich, satisfying, and creative lives. We believe that our students should have as many choices available after high school as possible. Therefore, our recommended program of study exceeds the graduation requirements of the Edmonds School District, and meets the entrance requirements for four-year state universities. These high expectations are balanced with high levels of personal support and creative exploration of the arts, to ensure student success.

The Achievement, Opportunity, and Service Community
The Achievement, Opportunity, and Service Community offers students and parents a traditional high school experience in a small school setting. Rigorous, innovative programs and an outstanding staff enhance this experience. Challenging core and advanced courses, a diverse elective program, and an emphasis on community service are successful elements of our small school.

To foster personalization and academic success for our students, the staff of our school has implemented four exciting programs. All students are involved in an advisory group where they receive academic guidance, learn leadership skills, and complete a community service project.

Source: Used by permission of Greg Schwab, principal, Mountlake Terrace High School.

The academies at Mountlake Terrace attempt to respond to different orientations toward learning, making them particularly attractive as personalized learning communities.

Research on Smaller Learning Communities

Creating smaller, personalized schools within an existing large school involves understanding student interests and needs, creating smaller units or academies of 100 to 400 students relating to those needs, allowing the smaller schools to adopt a distinctive theme, dividing faculty among teams that stay with students for two to four years, allocating some part (30 percent to 100 percent) of the school day to academy teams, and allowing students to choose a theme or change teams as they learn.

A body of research suggests that smaller schools are associated with higher achievement, lower absentee rates, and higher rates of college application. Lorna Jimerson (2006) has collapsed studies of smaller, or conversion, high schools into 10 benefits that accrue with small size:

1. Greater participation in extracurricular opportunities
2. Safer schools
3. More feelings of belonging among students
4. More individualized instruction
5. Easier time implementing good teaching methods
6. Better feelings among teachers about their work
7. Increased tendency toward mixed-ability classes can avoid condemning some students to low expectations
8. Increased prevalence of multiage classes can promote personalized learning and encourage positive social interactions
9. Smaller districts limit bureaucracy
10. Increased number of grade levels in one school can alleviate problems with transition to new schools

From these types of reviews and studies, a picture emerges that smaller schools are more serious about learning, more collaborative in relationships, and less mechanical in administration (Newmann & Wehlage, 1995).

Breaking large schools into smaller ones also creates natural group-
ings for comparative research. Linda Darling-Hammond and her colleagues (Darling-Hammond, Ancess, & Ort, 2002) studied changes in
student outcomes when a large, urban high school in New York was
replaced by six smaller schools designed to personalize learning. The
Coalition Campus Schools Project (CCSP) compared measures of success
for the original Julia Richmond High School (1992–1993) with the
average same measures for the six smaller, personalized schools that
replaced it (1995–1996), as shown in Figure 7.3.

FIGURE 7.3
Comparison of Student Outcomes at Large and Small Schools

Measure	Julia Richmond High School (1992–1993)	CCSP Average (1995–1996)
Average daily attendance	72%	86.2%
Incident rates (disciplinary)	3.3	1.2
1-year dropout rates	6.1	1.2
Students with reading gains	52.4%	56.9%

11th grade passing RCT or regents
  In reading
  In mathematics
  In writing
	79%
	57.5%
	75.2%
		80%
		76.6%
		71.4%

LEP students with adequate language gains	53%	91.2%

Source: Adapted from Darling-Hammond, Ancess, & Ort, 2002

A similar pattern of outcomes appears when the percentage of CCSP
students (general education) passing Regents Examinations is compared
to percentages passing in schools demographically similar to CCSP but
conventional in structure and size, as shown in Figure 7.4. Even when

FIGURE 7.4
Comparison of Pass Rates on Regents Exams

Subject	Percentage of Students Passing Regents Examinations, 1996–1997	
	Similar School	CCSP Average
Reading	82.4	93.6*
Writing	70.4	85*
Mathematics	81.2	79.4

*$p < .001$

Source: Adapted from Darling-Hammond, Ancess, & Ort, 2002

differences are not statistically significant, they are systemic. That is, all the differences point in a positive direction.

Further research adds to the weight of evidence in favor of personalized learning in smaller settings. Valerie Lee and her colleagues (Lee & Smith, 1994) at the University of Wisconsin studied how 30 practices associated with 820 high schools influenced scores on the National Assessment of Educational Progress as reported in the National Education Longitudinal Study database. High schools that implemented more than three of the 30 practices reported consistently higher achievement than conventional schools operating within a centralized, bureaucratic structure. Furthermore, schools adopting three or more of the following restructuring practices scored higher than more conventional schools:

- Students keep the same homeroom throughout high school
- Emphasis on staff solving school problems
- Parents volunteer in school
- Interdisciplinary teaching teams
- Independent study in English and social studies
- Independent study in math and science
- Mixed-ability classes in math and science

- Cooperative learning focus
- Student evaluation of teachers
- Flexible planning time for teacher teams
- Flexible time for classes

These restructuring practices are also characteristic of smaller-schools initiatives. In Lee's analysis (Lee & Smith, 1994), students in smaller schools also scored higher than students in larger schools.

Still, it would be a mistake to assume that smaller is necessarily better—that converting a ponderous comprehensive high school into academies will change student performance, student behavior, or even school climate. Smaller settings allow a school community to manage the change process in ways that encourage personalization. After carefully watching the conversion decision at North Eugene High School in Oregon, Bob Pearlman (2005) observed the following:

> Large high school conversion requires design, implementation, and effective change management to bring about successful new small schools and a new culture of teaching and learning. District leadership and support, and effective small school leadership, is crucial.
>
> Small school advocates no longer have the easy case statement of just pointing to disastrous large, comprehensive high schools. Instead they, like the educational leaders at North Eugene High School, will have to make the whole case—design, implementation (execution), leadership, and curriculum make a difference.

The process of developing a personalized learning community begins with assembling a shared vision of what the school will be—for students, teachers, administrators, and community members. Once created, a good vision statement gives all participants a way to guide and regulate themselves as they begin to work through the options toward real choices.

Applying a Shared Vision

Developing a mission statement can be a drab activity carried out by a small group of people preparing for the arrival of a school accreditation team. Or in a smaller, personalized school, the vision statement and mission may emerge from long deliberation among all members of the school community, who then apply them as useful tools to daily issues: the structure of the schedule, course design, discipline systems, and personal learning plans. A group of writers associated with the Big Picture Company in Providence explained:

> What is most striking about a school with a coherent intellectual mission is that adults and students tend to use the same language in talking about the school. The mission is accessible to all, including bilingual and special needs students. It is also assessable—students understand they must demonstrate the skills and understandings that the mission calls for. (Riordan, Roche, Goldhammer, & Stephen, 1999, p. 15)

In short, a serious mission statement stands at the center of school life, helping all members plan their path, apply their learning, and assess their growth.

When the words and ideas embodied by the mission or vision statement appear in daily conversation, the school has probably developed an organizing framework for understanding and directing itself. For example, the mission of the Fenway High School in Boston asserts personalization as a central tenet:

> Fenway High School's mission is to create a socially committed and morally responsible community of learners that values its students as individuals. Fenway's goal is to encourage academic excellence and habits of mind, self-esteem, and leadership development among all the school's students. (Coalition of Essential Schools, n.d.)

One student confirmed the influence of the mission in a group interview, working from experience as much as abstraction:

> We are a community. We know each other. I still have the same people in advisory I had in 9th grade. People help. Fenway is a school for everybody. You are welcome to be different. We are all getting what we need, but we have different needs.

Emerging in different voices throughout the school, the mission creates the vocabulary that lets the school examine itself and set new directions.

When the number of converted schools within a district is large, a vision may grow quite elaborate, so it includes ideas that justify a range of different options for students. When six smaller schools replaced Skyview High School in Mapleton, Colorado, the mission (found on the Skyview Web site at www.mapleton.us/schools/skyviewsenior.html) was drawn up to emphasize commonalities but also permit the growth of different approaches to personalization:

> The mission of Skyview High Schools, a dynamic, innovative, and learning-focused family of schools, which embraces the diversity of our population, thrives on a foundation of integrity and positive relationships, and commits to the success of every student, is to guarantee that every student realizes dreams, develops productive habits of learning, a positive sense of self-worth and fulfillment, unleashes potential, and contributes meaningfully to our community and world through an educational system characterized by: Leadership at all levels that promotes responsible decision making; high academic standards and expectations for all students; a challenging, relevant, and rigorous selection of learning opportunities based on student interests and abilities; mutually beneficial partnerships; and a safe environment of encouragement and enthusiasm that nurtures the whole person.

Because Skyview has organized the framework of student portfolios to reflect the school's mission, the portfolios show how deeply a shared vision permeates school life. Each student voice is distinctive. One student stated in the personal section of her portfolio:

> I have been more involved in my classes and the school. I have helped my friends and become more loyal to them. I have gotten to improve in writing papers for different purposes. That was a big growth for me. But the one thing better than that is that I now have more self-confidence and courage to stand up for what is right.

In a personalized high school, personal growth goals should not overwhelm intellectual goals in the school mission. To operate consistently between middle school and college, a personalized school should emphasize a clear intellectual mission. Riordan and colleagues (1999) have listed six features to watch for in a personalized high school mission statement:

- Common core goals across the curriculum
- Curriculum integration across vocational and academic areas
- Cross-cutting standards developed and assessed internally
- Assessment focused on what students understand and can do
- Field experiences that connect with academics and vice versa
- Program standards that allow all students to qualify for four-year colleges

In their conception, cross-cutting goals and standards support integration and assessment across the subject areas, and field experiences reinforce the importance of academics in life and college admissions.

The Need for Defined Autonomy

As high schools adapt to better meet the needs, interests, talents, and aspirations of their students, perhaps the most restrictive influences come from outside the school. Schools often organize themselves as hierarchical structures because the hierarchical structures that control them seem to grow more influential and powerful as they gain distance from the school. As some research has shown, however, the factors that improve student learning are largely local, embedded in student experience: teachers, curriculum, and parents. Distant factors—federal, state, and local policies, for example—have little measurable effect on how or how well students learn (Wang, Haertel, & Wahlberg, 1993). Nevertheless, external powers in the public sphere do not hesitate to wade into school decision making whenever powerful people outside the school think they have recognized an untended problem. Mandates and required procedures rain down, eating up instructional time and interrupting administrative priorities. When mandates and requirements are linked to funding, no amount of nodding, dodging, or fudging compliance can blunt the impact on school climate and the spirit of innovation.

To compound the impact of diversions from the outside, some external requirements are contradictory. A state department of education may be pursuing the flexible recommendations of *Breaking Ranks*, while the federal department of education is requiring a uniform process of testing for all students. A school may institute interdisciplinary teams, just to discover that a state regulation requires a teacher license in a specific subject area for any teacher working with students in that area. Because distant powers are distant from the problems and opportunities teachers and administrators face every day, they tend to impose solutions that are simplistic, misguided, impractical, political, or inconsistent with the established trajectory of change. External demands often impose uniformity on the system, preventing high schools from exploring more effective programs that respond to individual differences.

For a smaller learning community to thrive, it has to negotiate the limits of control from external forces so teachers, administrators, students, and community members recognize what they are able to do to deepen personalized learning and what they have to do to show others operational boundaries. High schools cannot begin to improve learning for their students unless they can manage the factors that create success. Because those factors are all local to the individual, defining autonomy in areas close to the student experience gives a faculty a chance to modify failing systems. The Center for Collaborative Education in Boston has made a point of defining areas of autonomy for several pilot schools in the city.

Pilot Schools' defining philosophy is that if schools are provided maximum control over their resources to create innovative education programs in exchange for increased accountability, student engagement and performance will improve. Five areas of autonomy exist in Pilot Schools: staffing, budget, curriculum and assessment, governance, and schedule. Through autonomy, Pilot Schools possess increased decision-making power to best meet the needs of their students and create the conditions that realize each school's respective mission and vision. Because the pilot schools are as small as 120 students, collaborative management is feasible.

Personalized high schools need to create new processes and structures to manage their autonomy, and those processes need to be consistent with the school's vision and mission. Poland High School in Poland, Maine, created a decision-making process based on consensus for all internal issues (except those covered by federal, state, or local regulations, such as school board policy and administrative policy).

The governance structure at Poland High ties together teams that develop and monitor seven aspects of school life:

- *The Student Event Team (SET)*. The SET's mission is to plan, publicize, execute, and coordinate events and activities that promote a positive school culture, consistent with the school's mission.
- *Student Involvement and Action Team (SIA)*. SIA will make recommendations regarding issues that directly affect students.
- *Student Judicial Board*. This team hears and adjudicates behavior problems.
- *Teaching and Learning*. Teaching and Learning will make recommendations regarding issues that directly affect teaching and learning in the building—for example, the curriculum.
- *Full Faculty*. A gathering of all teachers to discuss and make a recommendation.
- *The Filter Group*. The Filter Group reviews all proposals and decides which subcommittee (or administration) to send them to for discussion and if the issue affects grades 7 to 12 or grades 9 to 12.
- *The Vision Keepers*. The Vision Keepers meet weekly and make binding decisions on matters in areas not covered by federal, state, or

local regulations, or school board policy and formal votes, based on proposals from the various subcommittees. The principal is present at every Vision Keepers meeting, and no decisions are made in the absence of the principal.

Every team or committee has at least one student. Several include a school board or community member. Any member of the school community may submit a proposal to the Filter Group on a form the school has developed. If Filter Group members are unsure about the proposal's need for action, then they can ask the requestor to get at least 10 signatures supporting the proposal. If the Filter Group decides that the proposal concerns a real need in the school that merits attention, then the group decides which governance committee will review the proposal. After the appropriate governance committee explores the proposal, members send it to the Vision Keepers group for a binding decision.

Although the governance structure is democratic, the process of making a decision is consensual. Instead of voting a proposal up or down, teams, committees, and other groups survey the participants using the Fist-to-Five technique developed by the American Youth Foundation, as explained in Figure 7.5. Any show of a fist represents a lack of consensus. Any show of five fingers reflects a level of enthusiasm that implies willingness to actively work on the issue. By using consensus rather than a majority vote, the Poland system encourages discussion among all group members, leading to a decision with which all, at the very least, have agreed to comply.

Wrestling with Time

For more than 15 years, high school educators have been searching for ways to decrease the periodic mayhem that occurs in the halls seven times a day in an eight-period high school schedule. Rettig and Canady came to the rescue in 1999, offering a slew of optional high school schedules for consideration. Most of the options feature longer blocks of time that can, according to Mistretta and Polansky (1997), facilitate the following goals:

FIGURE 7.5
Building Consensus Using Fist-to-Five

Purpose of This Document: To explain and clarify the voting and group decision-making procedure used at PRHS/ BMWMS [Poland Regional High School/Bruce M. Whittier Middle School] for new and veteran members of the school community.

Background: When a group comes to consensus on a matter, it means that everyone in the group can support the decision; they don't all have to think it's the best decision, but they all agree they can live with it. Whenever a group is discussing a possible solution or coming to a decision on any matter, Fist-to-Five, developed by the American Youth Foundation, is a good tool to determine what each person's opinion is at any given time.

In Practice: To use this technique, the facilitator restates a decision the group may make and asks everyone to show his or her level of support. Each person responds by showing a fist or a number of fingers that corresponds to their opinion.

Fist	A no vote—a way to block consensus. I need to talk more about the proposal and require changes for it to pass. A fist also implies a responsibility to engage in conversations with invested parties, moving toward consensus.
1 Finger	I have serious reservations but I can live with it as it is. I will respect, not obstruct, implementation of the proposal. I may like to offer a cautionary or advisory remark prior to implementation.
2 Fingers	I'm not in total agreement but feel comfortable to let this decision or proposal pass without further discussion.
3 Fingers	I have minor reservations but can support the idea.
4 Fingers	I think it's a good idea/decision and would actively support it.
5 Fingers	I feel strongly about this idea and feel that it is essential to our mission and vision. I would be willing to work actively toward implementation.

Additional Clarifications:
• Fist-to-Five will be the typical decision-making process for official committees and governance groups at PRHS and Whittier, including the full faculty, the Vision Keepers Governance Subcommittees, Learning Areas, and Roundtable Teams.
• Before potentially contentious full-faculty votes, facilitators are encouraged to allow small-group processing and discussion time.
• Fist-to-Five will NOT be used for elections, for straw polls, or for Performance Archive conferences. Work Agreement and Union decisions/votes are outside the purview of our norms.
• The full faculty may choose to use a decision-making process other than Fist-to-Five to resolve a particular issue if the faculty votes—Fist-to-Five—to support that alternative process.
• Before giving an "absolutely no" vote (displaying a fist), a group member is encouraged, but not required, to share his/her concerns with the full group. After voting "no" the person should be given the opportunity to share the reasons that he or she cannot live with the proposal. He or she also has the right to silence ("to pass") at that point in time. In either circumstance, the dissenting party must be willing to meet with proposers/proponents of the idea outside the given meeting to try to work toward consensus
• If there are several 1s and 2s, then further discussion is recommended before the proposal is implemented.

Note: This tool is adapted from Fletcher, A. (2002). FireStarter Youth Power Curriculum: Participant Guidebook. Olympia, WA: Freechild Project. It was originally developed by the American Youth Foundation.

Source: Used by permission of William Doughty, Principal, Poland Regional High School.

- Decreasing class changes and transitions during the school day.
- Reducing duplication and inefficiency.
- Lowering the number of students a teacher sees each day.
- Cutting down the number of courses a teacher must prepare for each day.
  - Limiting fragmentation.
  - Providing flexible instructional environments.
  - Allowing time variations among content areas.
  - Focusing teacher time to promote creativity in the classroom.
  - Increasing planning time for teachers.
  - Adding instructional time for students.
  - Limiting disruptions and improving engagement.

Goals such as these have changed the high school day in many schools, and they have also improved student achievement, attendance, and discipline referrals. In a personalized high school, modified block schedules have been used to increase engagement, making time for personal learning plans, advisories, project-based learning, and personalized assessment.

Still, block scheduling may not be the perfect answer to the problem of time in a personalized high school. Three major approaches to scheduling a day emerged from the scheduling flurry 10 years ago: the conventional seven- to eight-period day; an intensive block schedule of four courses in two semesters (4 x 4); and the alternating block, with six to eight courses meeting every other day. Combinations of these three basic plans proliferated, aiming to accommodate subject areas that benefit from different amounts of time and students who also have their preferences. Overall, the results of these uncommon innovations in high school practices have made a difference in the ways schools work. A multitude of variations and combinations of these three forms were explored by Cotton (2002) and the LAB at Brown University (1998). Because so many variations exist, it is often relatively easy to develop a schedule that fits faculty and student needs, particularly if they have been active in designing their days and weeks.

Virtually any block scheduling format increases opportunities for teacher–student interactions through projects, field trips, and scheduled advising. In a smaller learning community, variations of block scheduling also create flexibility for academies, teams, or schools within schools. At the Urban Academy, one of the smaller schools bred by the breakup of Julia Richmond High School, the faculty has experimented with curriculum-driven scheduling, allowing teachers to design a new schedule each semester, based on the needs of different courses and patterns of achievement among students.

> Scheduling the week to reflect differences among courses defines core values at the school. . . . Toward the end of each semester—in January and in June—the staff reviews the previous term's work. Both courses and the schedule are assessed through the lens of student achievement. Were there noticeable gaps, not enough time for revision support work, too few "lab" classes to support the specific academic needs of students, not enough opportunities for field trips? Did teachers have time to do what they planned? Did the time of day particular classes were offered (e.g., first period, last period) matter? In short, did the structure created work as intended? Did we get what we wanted? (Cook, 2004)

Any schedule aiming to personalize learning should include time for innovation and deliberation within the faculty, as well as advising, project-based learning, and community experience. Without time, change is impossible.

Interactive Leadership

No one can doubt the necessity of leadership in a changing school. In a large, conventional high school, one leader—the principal—has the final word and is accountable to the school board and superintendent for whatever happens in the school. In a smaller school, however, leadership can spread throughout the learning community, energizing the whole school and spreading responsibility widely. At the very least, students actively lead project-based learning teams as well as parents and teachers through portfolio review and roundtable exhibitions. Advisors lead their students from blurry goals and uncertain skills to clear aspirations—and even passion for particular fields of study. Teachers lead their students through project development and problem solving. Administrators lead multiple teams in decision making and problem solving. Ray Proulx, a superintendent from Vermont, calls this phenomenon "leadership density," a phenomenon in which many people are providing leadership for many different initiatives—simultaneously—on behalf of a shared vision.

In a series of close observations in five Vermont high schools moving toward student-centered learning, researchers noticed a pattern of leadership that did not resemble hierarchical leadership from the top (Clarke et al, 2000). Instead of occurring through memos, mandates, and meetings, leadership in these changing schools emerged from personal interactions among many people that took place naturally during the day. Some call these leadership exchanges conversations (Cushman, 1997). Usually, these interactions crossed the boundaries that divide people into specialties and offices.

Mapping the pattern of these interactions revealed that making connections across the boundaries of role and status ensured that the decisions made would have at least two proponents from different parts of the system. Interactions were most vigorous in high schools with very active change initiatives. A pattern of continuous interaction across all the hierarchical separations from classroom to superintendent's office ensured that an innovation could remain viable.

In the Vermont study of high school innovation, leadership permeated the whole system, at least in respect to the changes being developed. During the period of change, leadership at different levels of the system was simultaneous rather than sequential. Two teachers at one high school created the school's first standards-based unit, asking each student to develop a land-use plan for a scrap of Vermont geography torn from a topographic map. To create and revise the unit, various elements of the schools worked together:

- The state Department of Education offered a stipend for teachers who would use the new state standards to design examples.
- The superintendent imported a field-based master's degree program with a focus on curriculum design.
- The local university supplied teaching interns to assist master teachers with course development.
- The principal initiated a schoolwide restructuring initiative.
- The teacher developed and revised the new unit in a class of highly resistant students.
- The students field tested the project guides with varying degrees of enthusiasm, helping the teacher and intern rethink their design.
- On exhibition day, all students presented their proposals to a mock planning commission consisting of teachers, university instructors, and community members.

The exuberant mood that then infected the class celebrated leadership by all, applied simultaneously across the boundaries that usually divide a high school into bureaucratic chambers.

As much research has shown, however, principal leadership remains crucial to any change effort. Someone in the school has to know how the process is working. Someone has to draw new leaders into new roles. And someone has to watch external relations with the board and community. In interviews with staff and faculty as they studied successful principals,

DiMartino and Miles (2006) observed four attributes shared by principals during school change:

> (1) In framing a vision for their school, each principal was driven by deeply rooted care and concern for every student in the school. (2) When the principals were seeking to work collaboratively with staff in sharing the leadership for the vision, they had the ability to empathize with the staff; in their willingness and ability to understand the various viewpoints of others, the principals demonstrated an uncommonly high level of self-confidence. (3) Implementing the strategies required that they become strong salespersons—initially for their ideas, but eventually for a collaboratively created vision for their school. (4) This all required that they have a very strong work ethic and an almost stubborn determination to succeed, while maintaining an orderly calm in the face of often bitter conflict. (DiMartino & Miles, 2006, p. 47)

Making students come first, supporting a diffused system of leaders, and holding steady through the storms that blow takes calm, courage, commitment, and thorough confidence in the directions a school has chosen to travel.

In addition to new roles for the principals, teachers in changing schools have begun to adopt new roles. By habit, most teachers in large high schools have confined leadership to their own classrooms, where a closed door can establish some autonomy. In a changing school, teachers must leave their classrooms and cross unbroken boundaries: leading an interdisciplinary team, managing the advising system, arranging professional development, or simply working with others to improve instruction. Teacher leaders may face substantial barriers in a large, impersonal high school where roles fit a hierarchical structure. In a smaller school, growth would not be possible without teacher leadership. Wallach and Lear's (2005) study of 17 comprehensive high schools evolving into 72 smaller learning communities revealed that teacher leadership was universal during the change process. Leadership roles were formally established, but fluid:

> All of the 17 conversions have created teacher-leadership roles in their small schools, although the roles continue to evolve in each of the small schools. Few written job descriptions existed in this transition period; indeed, understandings or agreements between and among teachers and building administrators appeared to be less important than daily routines in shaping teacher-leader roles. (Wallach & Lear, 2005, p. 9)

To preserve collegial cooperation, no teacher leaders in the 72 smaller schools had supervisory responsibility. To the extent that teacher leadership is professional leadership and flexibility is essential to growth, job descriptions may not prove useful at all. A team, academy, or smaller school aiming to respond to individual students may want to avoid tight roles and the appearance of hierarchy. Additionally, teacher leaders may be more influential if their leadership assignments are only partial; professional leadership depends on remaining active within the profession.

After 50 years of relative stasis within a conventional structure, stability and order have become primary virtues of comprehensive high schools. Change cannot occur in a perfectly orderly context—no more than life can thrive on a frozen planet. Change requires some turbulence. Change creates heat. Change brings strain to all who participate, because their lives are changing with the institutions they are rebuilding. Because they have built self-confidence in their traditional roles, they may lose confidence as their roles shift and grow. Conflict grows as individuals leave their accustomed ground and venture out with others into the unknown. In short, the experience of change in a personalized high school is deeply personal. An initiative may threaten to disintegrate almost daily as individuals lose their way. Consequently, leadership is essential in every aspect of daily work. Teamwork is vital. The only way to create new order is to focus with unvarying intensity on a single aim: engaging each student in learning how to use information to manage their own lives and the continuing growth of their communities.

Appendix

Rubric for Guiding and Assessing Projects in Fight for Your Rights

This appendix is a companion to the discussion of the "Fight for Your Rights" project on pages 88–93. The rubric is used by the students to guide their project development and by the teacher to assess the final product.

NTHS American Studies
Fight for Your Rights
Human Rights Book Rubric

Student: _____
Evaluator: _____   Date: _____

Criteria	Unsatisfactory (Below Performance Standards)	Proficient (Minimal Criteria)	Advanced (Demonstrates Exceptional Performance)

Work Ethic	• Book is not completed on time
	• Book does not have a title or title is not appropriate
	• Book does not have a cover or the cover is not appropriate
	• Book is not in MLA format
	• Book does not include one or more of the following elements:
	  – A complete Table of Contents
	  – An overview/history of the movement
	  – A chronological overview of important events/dates with explanations and visual aids
	  – One or more of the required biographies
	  – One or more of the required pieces of literature (or one or more pieces is not analyzed)
	  – At least two original works of poetry (with explanations) that relate to the rights movement
	  – At least one visual aid on each page
	  – An MLA Works Cited page at the end of the book
		• Book is completed on time
		• Book has an appropriate title
		• Book has an appropriate cover
		• Book is in MLA format
		• Book includes the following elements:
		  – A Table of Contents with page numbers, brief explanations, and student authors
		  – An original overview/background of the movement
		  – An original chronological overview of important events/dates with explanations and visual aids
		  – One original biography per group member
		  – One piece of literature and analysis per group member (that is relevant to the movement)
		  – At least two original works of poetry (with explanations) that relate to the rights movement
		  – At least one visual aid on each page (with source/byline)
		  – An accurate MLA Works Cited page at the end of the book
			In addition to meeting the PROFICIENT criteria . . .
			• Title and cover of book are creative, unique, and engaging to the viewer
			• Book demonstrates an exceptional amount of effort, planning, and collaboration
			• Book is enhanced by the inclusion of additional elements such as analysis of relevant artwork, original pieces of artwork, discussion/analysis of relevant films, etc.

	0 ——— 20 ——— 25 ——— 30	35 ——— 38 ——— 40 ——— 42 ——— 44	45 ——————— 50

NTHS American Studies
Fight for Your Rights
Human Rights Book Rubric

Student: _____

Evaluator: _____   Date: _____

Criteria	Unsatisfactory (Below Performance Standards)	Proficient (Minimal Criteria)	Advanced (Demonstrates Exceptional Performance)
History Content	• Overview/background of the movement does not adequately cover its history and/or development • Many significant dates/events are absent from the chronological overview • Each date/event on the overview does not include a detailed paragraph, or the paragraphs do not adequately explain the events and/or their significance • One or more of the biographies is not focused on an individual who is relevant to the movement • One or more of the biographies does not adequately synthesize a variety of information from multiple sources • One or more of the biographies does not adequately discuss the individual's life and/or the individual's role in the movement • Many historical references are not accurate	• Overview/background of the movement adequately covers its history and development • Significant dates/events have been included in the chronological overview of the movement • Each date/event on the overview includes a detailed paragraph that effectively explains the event, as well as its significance • Each biography is focused on an individual who is relevant to the movement, which is clearly explained in the biography • Each biography effectively synthesizes a variety of information from multiple sources • Each biography effectively discusses the life of the individual and his or her role in the movement • All historical references are accurate	In addition to meeting the PROFICIENT criteria . . . . • Overview/background of the movement is insightful and thorough • Chronological overview and event explanations are exceptionally detailed and well-chosen • Biographies demonstrate an advanced understanding of the individual's contributions to the rights movement • Historical connections and insights are exceptional, and are consistently demonstrated throughout the book
	0 ------- 30 ------- 50 ------- 60	70 ------- 73 ------- 78 ------- 83 ------- 88	90 ------------- 100

NTHS American Studies
Fight for Your Rights
Human Rights Book Rubric

Student: _____
Evaluator: _____   Date: _____

Criteria	Unsatisfactory (Below Performance Standards)	Proficient (Minimal Criteria)	Advanced (Demonstrates Exceptional Performance)
English Content	• Each piece of literature included in the book is not adequately analyzed for its relevance to the rights movement • Each analysis (of literature) does not incorporate enough relevant and/or interesting information about the author(s) • Each analysis does not adequately analyze a literary device used by the author(s) • Each original work of poetry does not adequately incorporate at least two poetic devices • Each original work of poetry is not accompanied by an adequate explanation of its purpose, its connection to the rights movement and/or the poetic devices being used	• Each piece of literature has a correlation to the rights movement • Each piece of literature is effectively analyzed for its relevance to the rights movement • Each analysis discusses the author, as well as the author's relevance to the movement • The explanation of each piece of literature effectively analyzes at least one literary device • Each original work of poetry effectively incorporates at least two poetic devices • Each original work of poetry is accompanied by an effective explanation of its purpose, its connection to the rights movement, as well as the poetic devices being used	In addition to meeting the PROFICIENT criteria . . . . • The analysis of each piece of literature is insightful and thorough • The analysis of each piece of literature thoroughly and thoughtfully analyzes many literary devices used by the author(s) • Original works of poetry are creative and well-written, leaving a lasting impression on the reader • Original works of poetry effectively incorporate many poetic devices, demonstrating advanced poetry-writing skills • Thoughtful connections are made between the pieces of literature and/or the poetry and the rights movement
	0 ------- 30 ------- 50 ------- 60	70 ------- 73 ------- 78 ------- 83 ------- 88	90 ------- 100

NTHS American Studies
Fight for Your Rights
Human Rights Book Rubric

Student: _____

Evaluator: _____   Date: _____

Criteria	Unsatisfactory (Below Performance Standards)	Proficient (Minimal Criteria)	Advanced (Demonstrates Exceptional Performance)
Written Communication	• Transitions are consistently ineffective or absent • Vocabulary, word choice, and sentence structure are not varied and/or appropriate in all written pieces • Much of the writing is not clear, coherent, developed, or organized • There are many errors in spelling, grammar and punctuation, which interfere with the effectiveness of the book • There are many comma splices, fragments and/or run-on sentences in the written pieces • Arguments are frequently not supported with evidence or detailed references to historical events • Writing is not professional or informative in nature • Written pieces are not engaging and often lack creativity	• Transitions are smooth in each piece of writing • Vocabulary, word choice, and sentence structure are varied and appropriate in written pieces • Written pieces are generally clear, coherent, developed and organized • Written pieces contain few errors in spelling, grammar, and punctuation, which do not interfere with the effectiveness of the book • Written pieces contain few comma splices, fragments and/or run-on sentences • Arguments are supported with detailed references to historical events or other pieces of evidence • Writing is generally professional and informative in nature (except for original works of poetry) • Written pieces are creative and engaging	In addition to meeting the PROFICIENT criteria . . . . • Transitions are advanced, skillfully moving the reader through each piece of writing • Vocabulary, word choice, and sentence structure are advanced and effective in each piece of writing • Writing is engaging, creative, and very well-developed • Writing effectively integrates research with the student's own commentary and analysis • Writing is virtually free from errors in spelling, grammar, and punctuation
	0 ------- 30 ------- 50 ------- 60	70 ------- 73 ------- 78 ------- 83 ------- 88	90 -------------------- 100

Student: _____
Evaluator: _____   Date: _____

NTHS American Studies
Fight for Your Rights
Human Rights Book Rubric

Criteria	Unsatisfactory (Below Performance Standards)	Proficient (Minimal Criteria)	Advanced (Demonstrates Exceptional Performance)
Critical Thinking	• Minimal sense of cohesion and consistency • Book is not always appropriate for its audience • Book design is not effectively laid out and/or organized in a professional manner • Biographies, literature selections, and other pieces do not effectively represent the breadth of the topic • In-text citations are not accurately included when necessary, or are not in MLA format • Works Cited is not formatted appropriately • Written pieces do not effectively synthesize information from a variety of sources • Book does not demonstrate an understanding of the topic • Visuals are not effective in enhancing the book	• Book has a sense of cohesion and consistency • Book is appropriate for its audience • Book design is effectively laid out & organized in a professional manner • Biographies, literature selections, and other pieces represent the breadth of the topic • In-text citations are accurately included when necessary (in MLA format)—not foot/end notes • Works Cited is formatted appropriately • Written pieces effectively synthesize information from a variety of sources, demonstrating an understanding of the topic • Visuals are effective in enhancing the book	In addition to meeting the PROFICIENT criteria . . . . • Organization/layout of the book is highly creative and/or unique • All pieces in the book enhance the breadth and depth of the topic, demonstrating careful planning in both the selection and execution • In-text citations and Works Cited are flawless
	0 ------- 30 ------- 50 ------- 60	70 ------- 73 ------- 78 ------- 83 ------- 88	90 ------- 100

REFERENCES

Armstrong, S. (2002, February 11). Geometry in the real world: Students as architects. *Edutopia.* Retrieved August 5, 2007, from http://www.edutopia.org/geometry-real-world-students-architects

Ball, A. (2003, August 5). The Montana Heritage Project: What we once were, and what we could be. *Edutopia.* Retrieved August 19, 2007, from http://www.edutopia.org/montana-heritage

Berry, C. R. (2007, January). *School consolidation and inequality* (Harris School working paper: Series 07.02). Chicago: Harris School of Public Policy, University of Chicago.

Big Picture Company. (2001). *2000–2001 Met portfolio.* Retrieved August 14, 2007, from http://www.bigpicture.org/publications/MetPortfolios/MetPortfolio0001.pdf

Bloom, M. R., & Lafleur, B. (1999). *Turning skills into profit: Economic benefits of workplace education programs.* Retrieved August 20, 2007, from http://www.conferenceboard.ca/education/pdf/Skills_Profits.pdf

Boyer, E. (1993, March). *In search of community.* Presentation at the ASCD Annual Conference, Washington, DC.

Brown, J. S., Collins, A., & Duguid, S. (1989). Situated cognition and the culture of learning. *Educational Researcher, 18*(1), 32–42.

Clarke, J. (1992). The profession of teaching. In T. Fulwiler & A. W. Biddle (Eds.), *A community of voices: Reading and writing in the disciplines* (pp. 843–846). New York: Macmillan.

Clarke, J. (2003a). *Changing systems to personalize learning.* Providence, RI: Education Alliance at Brown University.

Clarke, J. (2003b). Personalized learning and personalized teaching. In J. DiMartino, J. Clarke, & D. Wolk (Eds.), *Personalized learning: Preparing high school students to create their futures* (pp. 69–86). Lanham, MD: Scarecrow Press.

Clarke J., & Agne, R. (1997). *Interdisciplinary high school teaching: Strategies for integrated learning.* Boston: Allyn & Bacon.

Clarke, J., Bossange, J., Erb, C., Gibson, D., Nelligan, B., Spencer, C., & Sullivan, M. (2000). *Dynamics of change in high school teaching: A study of innovation in five Vermont professional development schools.* Providence, RI: LAB at Brown University.

Clarke, J., Frazer, E., DiMartino, J., Fisher, P., & Smith, P. (2003). Making learning personal: Educational practices that work. In J. DiMartino, J. Clarke, & D. Wolk (Eds.), *Personalized learning: Preparing high school students to create their futures* (pp. 173–194). Lanham, MD: Scarecrow Press.

181

Coalition of Essential Schools. (n.d.) *Fenway High School* [Web page]. Retrieved August 16, 2007, from http://www.essentialschools.org/cs/schools/view/ces_sp/215

Cognition and Technology Group at Vanderbilt. (1990). Anchored instruction and its relationship to situated cognition. *Educational Researcher, 19*(5), 2–10.

Cook, A. (2004). *Time matters: Curriculum-driven scheduling: Urban Academy High School.* Retrieved November 15, 2006, from http://www.jrec.org/JREC_timematters.pdf

Cotton, K. (2002). Introduction. *Block scheduling: Definitions, effects, and support needs.* Retrieved August 20, 2007, from www.nwrel.org/scpd/sslc/descriptions/granby/pdfs/block_schedule_paper.pdf

Cushman, K. (1997, March). Essential leadership in the school change process. *Horace, 13*(4).

Daniels, E. & Arapostathis, M. (2005). What do they really want? *Urban Education (40),* 34-50.

Darling-Hammond, L., Ancess, J., & Ort, S. (2002). Reinventing high school: Outcomes of the Coalition Campus Schools Project. *American Educational Research Journal, 39*(3), 639–673.

Datesman, N. (2006, March 23). *Who asked us?—Haunted by 9th grade: A moral tale for all you high-schoolers.* Retrieved November 7, 2006, from http://news.newamericamedia.org/news/view_article.html?article_id=6ae7bd93af3496b1c69cbaba5bed7c68

DiMartino, J., & Castaneda, A. (2007, April). Assessing applied skills. *Educational Leadership, 64*(7), 38–42.

DiMartino, J., & Miles, S. (2006, June). Leadership at school: How to get the job done. *Principal Leadership, 6*(4), 47–50.

Dunn, R., & Dunn, K. (1993). *Teaching secondary students through their individual learning styles: Practical approaches for grades 7–12.* Boston: Allyn & Bacon.

Edutopia. (2002, February 11). Design for learning: The schools for 2050 project. Retrieved August 19, 2007, from http://www.edutopia.org/mountlake-terrace-schools-2050-project

Fulwiler, T. (1987). *The journal book.* Portsmouth, NH: Boynton/Cook.

Furger, R., & Shaffner, M. (2004, August 19). An incredible journey: Educators take on the charter school challenge. *Edutopia.* Retrieved August 5, 2007, from http://www.edutopia.org/an-incredible-journey

Gardner, H. (1991). *The unschooled mind: How children think and how schools should teach.* New York: Basic Books.

Illinois Mathematics and Science Academy. (2006). *Power of an idea: Problem-based Learning Network.* Retrieved August 20, 2007, from http://www.imsa.edu/programs/pbln/

Jimerson, L. (2006). *The hobbit effect: Why small works in public schools* (Rural Trust policy brief series on public education). Arlington, VA: Rural School and Community Trust.

Kolb, D. (1985). *Learning style inventory.* Boston, MA: McBer.

LAB, Northeast and Islands Regional Educational Laboratory. (1998). Block scheduling: Innovations with time (Themes in Education Series). Providence, RI: LAB, the Education Alliance at Brown University.

Learning Point Associates. (n.d.). School-to-Work Opportunities Act of 1994. Washington, DC: Center for Comprehensive School Reform.

Lee, V., Bryk, A., & Smith, J. (1993). The organization of effective secondary schools. In L. Darling-Hammond (ed.) *Review of Research in Education, 19,* 171–267.

Lee, V. & Smith, J. (1994). High school restructuring and student achievement. *Issues in Restructuring Schools, 7,* 1–5.

Lee, V., Smith, J., & Croninger, R. (1995a). How high school organization influences the equitable distribution of learning in mathematics and science. *Sociology of Education, 70,* 128–150.

Lee, V., Smith, J., & Croninger, R. (1995b). Another look at high school restructuring. *Issues in Restructuring Schools.* (Report No. 9). Madison, WI: Center on Organization and Restructuring of Schools.

McCarthy, B. (1990). Using the 4MAT system to bring learning styles to schools. *Educational Leadership, 48*(2), 31–37.

McLaughlin, M., & Blank, M. (2004, November 10). Creating a culture of attachment: A community-as-text approach to learning. *Education Week, 24*(11), 34–35.

Meier, D. (1995). *The power of their ideas.* Boston: Beacon Press.

Mistretta, G. M., & Polansky, H. B. (1997). Prisoners of time: Implementing a block schedule. *NASSP Bulletin, 81*(593), 23-31.

Mount Desert Island High School. (n.d.). *Mission statement.* Retrieved August 2, 2007, from http://mdihs.u98.k12.me.us/Accreditation/Mission_Statement/mission_statement.html

Mount Desert Island High School. (2005). *Personal learning plans at MDIHS* [Online document]. Retrieved July 30, 2007, from http://manila.mdihs.u98.k12.me.us/mdihslyons/stories/storyReader$51

National Association of Secondary School Principals. (2004). *Breaking Ranks II: Strategies for leading high school reform.* Reston, VA: Author.

National Education Association. (n.d.). Wyandotte High School, Kansas City. *NEA Priority Schools Newsletter.* Retrieved November 14, 2006, from www.nea.org/priorityschools/wyandottehs.html

National Science Teachers Association. (1990). Science/technology/society: A new effort for providing appropriate science for all: Teacher resources. Arlington, VA: Author. Available: http://www.nsta.org/positionstatement&psid=34

National Service Learning Clearinghouse. (n.d.). *Service learning is. . .* Scotts Valley, CA: ETR Associates. Retrieved August 20, 2006, from http://www.servicelearning.org/welcome_to_service-learning/service-learning_is/index.php

New Technology High School (NTHS). (2006). About NTHS [Web page]. Retrieved August 20, 2007, from http://www.newtechhigh.org/Website2007/index.html

Newmann, F. M. (1993). Crafting authentic instruction. *Educational Leadership, 50*(7), 8–12.

Newmann, F. M., & Wehlage, G. (1995). *Successful school restructuring: A report to the public and educators.* Madison, WI: Wisconsin Center for Education Research.

North Central Region Math/Science Education Collaborative. (n.d.). *Frogs! Frogs! Frogs!* [Web page]. Retrieved November 1, 2006, from http://www.mathsciencequest.org/frogs/

Organization for Economic Cooperation and Development (OECD). *Education at a Glance 2006.* Paris: Author.

Pearlman, B. (2005). *Making the case for conversions in 2005: It's getting harder* [Web page]. Retrieved November 23, 2006, from http://www.bobpearlman.org/BestPractices/North-EugeneHighSchool.htm#visit

Pearlman, B. (2006). *New models of learning for the 21st century: New Tech High School.* Retrieved August 8, 2007, from http://www.bobpearlman.org/modelschools.htm

Quint, J. (2006). *Meeting five critical challenges of high school reform: Lessons from research on three reform models.* New York: MDRC.

Rettig, M. D., & Canady, R. L. (1999, March). The effects of block scheduling. The School Administrator. Available: http://www.aasa.org/publications/

Riordan, R., Roche, B., Goldhammer, H., & Stephen, D. (1999). *Seeing the future: A planning guide for high schools*. Retrieved November 22, 2006, from http://www.bigpicture.org/publications/1999archives/SeeingTheFuture99.pdf

Rural School and Community Trust. (2003). *What does place-based learning look like? Examples of place-based learning portfolios*. Retrieved August 13, 2007, from http://files.ruraledu.org/rtportfolio/santafe/santafe_entry_directions3.htm

Schaff, T., Thackeray, T., & Alger, D. (2003). Students research seditious aliens, patriots, and elk in Roundup. *A narrative history of the Montana Heritage Project*. Retrieved August 13, 2007, from http://www.montanaheritageproject.org/index.php/sitehistory/siteHistory_entry/students-research-seditious-aliens-patriots-and-elk-in-roundup

Senge, P. (1990). *The fifth discipline*. New York: Doubleday.

Shorecrest High School. (n.d.). *A showcase of commitment and leadership*. Retrieved August 13, 2007, from http://schools.shorelineschools.org/shorecrest/facs/csweb/pages/showcase.html

Sizer, T. R. (1984). *Horace's compromise: The dilemma of the American high school*. Boston: Houghton Mifflin.

Snider, B. (2006). Building blocks: Fighting urban blight with teenage might. *Edutopia*. San Francisco: George Lucas Educational Foundation.

Steinberg, A. (2001). *Forty-three valedictorians: Graduates of the Met talk about their learning*. Boston, MA: Jobs for the Future.

Viadero, D. (1996, June 5). Teen culture seen impeding school reform [online article]. *Education Week*. Retrieved August 20, 2007, from http://www.edweek.org/ew/articles/1996/06/05/37peer.h15.html

Wallach, C. A., & Lear, R. (2005, Autumn). *A foot in two worlds: The second report on comprehensive high school conversions*. Seattle, WA: Small Schools Project, Bill and Melinda Gates Foundation. Retrieved August 20, 2007, from http://www.smallschoolsproject.org/PDFS/foot_full.pdf

Wang, M., Haertel, G., & Wahlberg, H. (1993). Toward a knowledge base for school learning. *Review of Education Research, 63*(3), 249-294.

Washor, E. (2003). When learning works. In J. DiMartino, J. Clarke, & D. Wolk (Eds.), *Personalized learning: Preparing high school students to create their futures* (pp. 1–16). Lanham, MD: Scarecrow Press.

Wheeling Jesuit University Center for Educational Technologies. (n.d.). *El Nino: The child returns*. Retrieved November 1, 2006, from http://www.cotf.edu/ete/modules/elnino/crsituation.html

Wiggins, G. (1993). *Educative assessment: Designing assessments to inform and improve student performance*. San Francisco: Jossey-Bass.

Wiggins, G., & McTighe, J. (2005). *Understanding by design* (expanded 2nd ed.) Alexandria VA: Association for Supervision and Curriculum Development.

INDEX

Page numbers followed by an *f* indicate figures.

ABOUT THE AUTHORS

Joseph DiMartino, founder and president of the Center for Secondary School Redesign, is a nationally recognized leader in the area of high school redesign. For nearly a decade, he served as director of the Secondary School Redesign Program at Brown University, where he gathered a diverse assembly of educators willing to experiment with high school personalization and student engagement. While at Brown, Joe wrote many articles, edited several books, and designed a series of workshops for high schools exploring reform. He is closely associated with NASSP, where he was one of the main architects of *Breaking Ranks II*. In recognition of his contribution to *Breaking Ranks II* and *Breaking Ranks in the Middle*, he received the NASSP Distinguished Service award in 2006. Joe has recently completed (along with Sherri Miles and Elaine Mangiante) the facilitators guide for the ASCD video series *High Schools at Work: Creating Student Centered Learning*. He has presented his research and writing extensively at national conferences, including those sponsored by ASCD. He can by reached by e-mail at joedimartino@ccsr.us or by phone at 401-828-0077.

John H. Clarke began teaching high school English in Massachusetts in 1966. He moved to Vermont in 1977 to teach secondary education and help run a teaching improvement program at the University of Vermont. He joined the research team working on the Secondary Initiative at LAB—the Education Alliance at Brown University—focusing on student engagement and high school personalization. Often with others, he has written or edited several books and many articles, focusing on high school change, high school teaching, and thinking strategies. He helped create a system of professional development schools in Vermont, linking teacher preparation and school improvement. For more than 20 years, he has worked to engage all students with the faculty and staff at Mount Abraham Union High School in Bristol, where he received an education recognition award in 2002. In the same year, he received the Vermont ASCD Leadership award. He continues to teach writing and thinking skills in Vermont. He can be reached by e-mail at jhclarke@gmavt.net or by phone at 802-453-2681.

Related ASCD Resources

At the time of publication, the following ASCD resources were available; for the most up-to-date information about ASCD resources, go to www.ascd.org. ASCD stock numbers are noted in parentheses.

Networks
Visit the ASCD Web site (www.ascd.org) and click on About ASCD. Go to the section on Networks for information about professional educators who have formed groups around topics such as "Service Learning/Experiential Learning" and "Problem-Based Learning." Look in the Network Directory for current facilitators' addresses and phone numbers.

Print Products
Awakening Genius in the Classroom by Thomas Armstrong (#198033)
The Big Picture: Education Is Everyone's Business by Dennis Littky and Samantha Grabelle (#104438)
The Classroom of Choice: Giving Students What They Need and Getting What You Want by Jonathan C. Erwin (#104020)
Classroom Instruction That Works: Research-Based Strategies for Increasing Student Achievement by Robert J. Marzano, Debra J. Pickering, and Jane E. Pollock (#101010)
Connecting with Students by Allen Mendler (#101236)
Designing Personalized Learning for Every Student by Dianne L. Ferguson, Ginevra Ralph, and Gwen Meyer (#101007)

Video
Classroom Management That Works Video Series: Sharing Rules and Procedures, Developing Relationships, and Fostering Student Self-Management (3 Videotapes and Facilitator's Guide #403344: DVD and Facilitator's Guide #604038)
High Schools at Work: Creating Student-Centered Learning (3 Videotapes with Facilitator's Guide #406117)
High Schools at Work: Personalizing the School (1 Tape with Facilitator's Guide #406119)
Motivation: The Key to Success in Teaching and Learning Video Series: Motivationally Anchored Instruction, Motivationally Anchored Classrooms, and Motivationally Anchored Schools (3 Videotapes and Facilitator's Guide #403344)
A Visit to a Motivated Classroom (Videotape and Viewer's Guide # 403384)

For more information, visit us on the World Wide Web (www.ascd.org), send an e-mail message to member@ascd.org, call the ASCD Service Center (1-800-933-ASCD or 703-578-9600, then press 2), send a fax to 703-575-5400, or write to Information Services, ASCD, 1703 N. Beauregard St., Alexandria, VA 22311-1714 USA.